CHARLES FINNEY

The Great Revivalist

Bonnie C. Harvey

BARBOUR
PUBLISHING

Other books in the "Heroes of the Faith" series:

Brother Andrew
Saint Augustine
Gladys Aylward
Dietrich Bonhoeffer
William and Catherine Booth
John Bunyan
John Calvin
William Carey
Amy Carmichael
George Washington Carver
Fanny Crosby
Frederick Douglass
Jonathan Edwards
Jim Elliot
Billy Graham
C. S. Lewis
Eric Liddell
David Livingstone
Martin Luther
D. L. Moody
Samuel Morris

George Müller
Watchman Nee
John Newton
Florence Nightingale
Luis Palau
Francis and Edith Schaeffer
Charles Sheldon
Mary Slessor
Charles Spurgeon
John and Betty Stam
Billy Sunday
Hudson Taylor
William Tyndale
Corrie ten Boom
Mother Teresa
Sojourner Truth
John Wesley
George Whitefield
William Wilberforce
John Wycliffe
Free Indeed
Some Gave All

Published by Barbour Publishing, Inc., P.O. Box 719, Uhrichsville, OH 44683, www.barbourbooks.com

Cover illustration © Dick Bobnick.

Member of the
Evangelical Christian
Publishers Association

Published in the United States of America.
5 4 3

CHARLES
FINNEY

Affectionately dedicated to my son, Steven,
a devoted admirer of Charles Finney.

one

"M r. Finney, won't you pray for me by name?" With tear-filled eyes the judge tugged at Finney's coat-tail. He added, "And I will go to the 'anxious' seat."

A short time before, the judge, who sat on the New York State Court of Appeals, had opposed Finney on certain points of doctrine and method. The judge had written Finney requesting that he give a series of lectures especially suited to lawyers. One of the topics he suggested was that of eternal punishment for the wicked. The judge, and numerous other lawyers, did not think such punishment could be proved.

Finney had complied and in 1842 began a series of lectures in Rochester, New York. On an earlier evening during the series, the judge had told Finney that he was convinced that Finney had dealt successfully with the topic and "nothing can be said against it." Finney knew that the judge had been deeply impressed, but he sensed it was still too early to ask the judge to make a decision about the claims of the gospel.

But when several nights later Finney began to close his evening message, he feared that he had failed to persuade the large congregation, which included many lawyers. Neither had Finney noticed the judge in his customary seat. Perhaps, Finney thought, the judge had decided not to attend the meeting that night.

So when Finney, still standing in the pulpit, turned to see the judge yanking on his coat, he was quite startled. He quickly told the congregation what the judge had said. Many people began to weep and pray, some coming forward and kneeling in front of the pulpit. Others held their heads down, praying fervently.

By this time, the judge had come around in front of Finney and knelt down. As he did, a startled Finney noted "the lawyers arose almost en masse, and crowded into the aisles, and filled the open space in front, wherever they could get a place to kneel. The movement had begun without my requesting it; but I then publicly invited any, who were prepared to renounce their sins, and give their hearts to God, and to accept Christ and His salvation, to come forward, into the aisles, or wherever they could, and kneel down." Many people came forward and knelt down. Then Finney prayed and dismissed the meeting.

Since he preached every night, Finney had not been able to take time for his usual inquirers' meetings, held for people who wanted to ask questions and get more information about salvation. In spite of this, Finney realized, "I had been carefully laying the net around the whole mass of lawyers, and hedging them in, as I supposed, by a train of reasoning that they could not resist. I was aware that lawyers are accustomed to listen to argument, to feel the weight of a logically presented truth." Finney sensed at this point that "the vast majority of them were thoroughly convinced" of the truth about Christ, and he would now lead them to a decision.

Finney set up an appointment for inquirers on the next day. When he arrived, the room was nearly full, and he was surprised to see that the audience "was composed almost exclusively of the more prominent citizens." He was pleased to see a large number of lawyers being converted—including the penitent judge who was willing to sit in what Finney called the "anxious seat," a place for those who were anxious about their soul's salvation to come forward and sit during the service. Finney noted that "the judge was at their head as he had taken the lead in coming out on the side of Christ."

Charles Finney remained in Rochester for two months as the fire of revival spread throughout the area. In many churches, entire congregations were converted and transformed. In his inquirer meetings, Finney stressed entire consecration—that is, giving body, soul, possessions, and everything else to God to be used for His glory.

One incident, in particular, that touched him deeply concerned a lawyer he had just met. At the door of the church the man handed Finney a paper, and remarked, "I deliver this to you as a servant of the Lord Jesus Christ." Finney placed the paper in his pocket until after the meeting. Looking at it later that evening, he found the paper "to be a quit-claim deed, made out in regular order, and executed ready for delivery, in which he quit-claimed to the Lord Jesus Christ, all ownership of himself, and of everything he possessed."

Nearly everywhere Charles Finney preached, revival broke out. Entire communities were changed by the power of God. After Finney had preached in those communities, saloons closed, theft stopped, and all kinds of vice and evil came to an end. The revival fire of God swept through communities, cleansing everything in its path.

From 1825 to 1830, Charles Finney gained national attention through a spectacular series of revival meetings in cities in New York along the Erie Canal—Rome, Utica, Troy, and Rochester. His success made the issues he raised unavoidable. He was controversial due to the novel techniques he used to promote revivals: extended nightly meetings, exhortations by women, and "the anxious seat" to which seekers were invited for counsel and prayer. These meetings were characterized by speech that was tough, direct, popular, and undeniably based on the free will of the individual. Finney is often called the forerunner of modern revivalism. He was also influential in the beginnings of urban evangelism.

It has been said of Finney that he probably led more souls to Christ than any other man and that he spearheaded a revival in America which altered the course of history. Others have thought Finney to be the greatest evangelist since apostolic times.

Even if these claims are somewhat exaggerated, it is true that Finney had a tremendous impact on his age. God used him mightily in what is known as the Second Great Awakening. Finney also helped create a new style of evangelism in America. Because of his special training and background, he was able to present the gospel plainly and rationally. Through his unique preaching, Finney bridged the gap between the exuberant camp meeting and the local church, making the gospel message more easily understood and thus more acceptable.

Just who was the man about whom such amazing claims were made? Was he someone plucked from the masses of rough, uneducated frontiersmen of the nineteenth century? Or was he a person with a profound religious background who had been educated at one of the prestigious universities such as Harvard or Yale?

Finney himself would have been the first to admit that he did not fit either of these descriptions. He considered himself just an average, ordinary person. But he was a person with an inquiring mind. He was not satisfied with simple answers to profound questions. He had to discover the answers for himself. And he set out to do so after embarking in an entirely different direction.

two

The first white settlers in the tiny Connecticut town of Warren arrived shortly after 1643, not long after the state itself was settled. Situated in the lush grasslands of Litchfield County in the area known as the western highlands, the town's inhabitants were mostly farmers and craftsmen. The grasslands provided ideal pasture for livestock.

Sylvester Finney had farmed the land in Warren since he returned from fighting in the Revolutionary War. His father's name, Josiah Finney, appears in the public records of Litchfield County some years after Sylvester's birth date of July 26, 1701. Josiah and Sylvester's ancestors had migrated to the colonies from England before 1639. Sylvester's wife, Rebecca Rice, whom he married when he came back from the war, also came from English ancestors.

In 1792, Sylvester and his wife were still living in Warren. That year, on August 29, their seventh child, a son, was born. Oddly, the Finneys departed from their usual custom of giving their children biblical names; instead, they named their son Charles Grandison after the hero of Samuel Richardson's popular novel, *Sir Charles Grandison.*

The choice of a nonbiblical name for this son did not mean the family had turned from religion. In fact, Charles Finney's grandfather Josiah had taken an active part in the founding of the Congregational Church in their community in 1756. Josiah had donated some new property he had just purchased to the fledgling congregation; then he witnessed the church's beginning and organization in his living room. Nevertheless, the family into which Charles Finney was born seemed to be far removed from real Christianity. Years later, Charles admitted he had never heard anyone pray in his home.

When Charles was just two years old, the family struck out for greener pastures, moving to the wilderness area of Oneida County in western New York. This move was typical of the adventuresome spirit of the time. Sylvester simply loaded his worldly possessions into an oxcart and covered wagon and moved on to a new area where he and Rebecca hoped life would be better. The family lived in Kirkland, New York, and a little later, they moved on to Sackett's Harbor on the shores of Lake Ontario.

At the close of the eighteenth century, western New York State was quite undeveloped. New York was only fifth in population among the states in the young country —eclipsed by Virginia, Massachusetts, Pennsylvania, and North Carolina. The wilderness, too, was more rugged and extensive than in Connecticut's Litchfield County.

The primitive schools of western New York reflected their communities. They possessed few of the educational tools of Boston or other cities of the time. Teachers were usually college students on vacation who had to teach with only a handful of books: *Webster's Blueback Speller, Hodder and Pike's Arithmetic,* and *Jebedia More's Universal Geography.*

In this limited environment, Charles Finney received his early education. Despite the lack of educational and other advantages—perhaps because of this lack—Charles prospered from his spartan upbringing. He developed tenacity, self-discipline, and endurance that served him well throughout his life.

At the age of fourteen, Charles entered Hamilton Oneida Academy in Clinton, New York. The academy was located just a few miles from his father's farm. Named after Alexander Hamilton, a Revolutionary War hero and leader of the new American Republic, the school helped shape Charles from an impressionable young boy into a confident young adult. Although he studied for only two years at the academy, Charles benefitted from the teaching of Seth Norton, the principal and a professor at the school. Norton saw his young student's potential and encouraged him to pursue a classical education and music. As a result, Charles became proficient in Latin, Greek, and Hebrew, and learned to play the violoncello quite well. With the first money he ever earned, Charles purchased a musical instrument.

While at the academy, Charles most likely received his first religious impressions from a missionary to the American Indians named Samuel Kirkland. Since Kirkland lived in the vicinity of the academy, Charles got to know him, but whether he ever heard Kirkland preach is not known. Whatever the depth of his relationship with Kirkland, it did not seem to lead Charles toward God at the time.

Young Charles Finney proved to be an outstanding student and athlete. He had a powerful physique, and he excelled in everything he attempted. He enjoyed many sports and participated in the various activities at Hamilton Academy. Whether the sport was running, riding, or wrestling, Finney mastered it. Years later, someone reported of him, "When he was twenty, he excelled every man and boy he met, in every species of toil or sport. No man could throw him; no man could knock his hat off; no man could run faster, jump farther, leap higher, or throw a ball with greater force and precision." When his family moved to the shore of Henderson Bay, near Sackett's Harbor, he added to his accomplishments rowing, swimming, and sailing.

Charles also possessed a good mind, and when he finished his academy studies, he taught school in Hamilton. He was just sixteen years old and taught for the next three years.

His students were very fond of Charles, and as was customary then, he taught for five months, then continued his own education for the rest of the year. Charles's students thought there was nothing their teacher couldn't do. One student said of him, "There was nothing which anyone else knew that Mr. Finney didn't know, and there was nothing which anyone else could do that Mr. Finney could not do—and do a great deal better. He was the idol of his pupils." Another student referred to him as "a

15

splendid pagan—a young man rejoicing in his strength, proudly conscious of his physical and intellectual superiority to all around him."

Charles's personal appeal to people of all ages continued throughout his life. But since he was not a Christian during his teaching days, he became somewhat obnoxious to the local minister, the Reverend George Gale. Since the young people flocked after Charles (and his irreligious ways), the Reverend Gale sometimes found it difficult to counteract Charles's attractive personality with the claims of the gospel.

At the outset of the War of 1812, Charles determined to join the navy. So he traveled the short distance from his home at Sackett's Harbor to the Sackett Harbor Naval Base. The prevailing rumor was that the British would soon invade the country from the north by sea.

Arriving at the naval base, Charles encountered the worst moral standards he had ever witnessed. Offensive crudeness and profanity were commonplace. When a young prostitute stopped him on the street, the innocent country boy did not realize what was taking place. But when he understood the prostitute's intentions, he began to weep, brokenhearted at her way of life. When she realized his concern for her, she began to weep as well. Although he was not a Christian, Charles had no tolerance for dissipated living. Rejecting the idea of naval life, he returned to his home.

By the fall of 1812, Charles had moved to his birthplace, Warren, Connecticut. Here, he lived with an uncle and worked on the family farm to support himself. Since he had determined to further his education, he also studied at an institution of higher learning with the same self-discipline and tenacity he had displayed in the little country school as a boy.

While living at Warren, Charles heard the first effective preacher of his life. The Reverend Peter Starr pastored at Warren from 1771 to 1822. His method of expounding the Scriptures was to put four fingers of each hand in the Bible, marking his texts for the sermon. Then he proceeded from finger to finger opening the Scriptures. Certainly the fact of Starr's good education and sincere preaching had an effect on Charles, but even so, he never joined the church at Warren.

Through his uncle's persuasion, Charles joined the Warren Masonic Lodge, eventually becoming a master mason. After his conversion, Charles repudiated his masonic connections with some irritation.

In 1814, Charles left Warren to teach school in New Jersey. After staying there two years, he traveled farther south to continue his education. But his mother's health began to fail and his parents wanted to have him closer to home, so Charles moved back to Jefferson County, New York, where his parents lived. Because of love and concern for his mother, he planned to stay nearby, so he decided to enter the law offices of Squire Benjamin Wright in Adams, New York.

To everyone who knew him, Charles seemed to be in an enviable position. He had everything necessary to become an outstanding lawyer: personality, intellect, and connections. According to his plan, once he had been admitted to the bar, he would practice law for a time and then go into politics. No one doubted he would succeed.

Everyone who knew Charles Finney understood that whenever he decided to do something, he would let nothing stand in his way.

After a few years, Charles became a junior law partner with Judge Wright in the Adams office. He was twenty-nine years old, and in the little community, he drew constant attention. He was six-feet, two-inches tall and weighed one hundred eighty-five pounds. His eyes were a vivid blue, and his gaze penetrating. His eyes added a tone of seriousness to Charles's commanding presence. He was also known by Adams's young people as a good dancer.

Charles still knew very little about the Christian faith, admitting he was "as ignorant of religion as a heathen." He may have exaggerated his lack of understanding somewhat, but until that period in his life, he had never heard any preaching of the gospel on a regular basis. He was a doubter, a skeptic. The frontier boasted few spirited churches, and even fewer well-educated ministers who could present the gospel clearly so people could understand. Charles and his family were not religious rebels. They were simply oblivious to real Christianity. But before long, all that would change as God began to draw Charles to Himself.

three

While continuing his law studies in Adams, New York, Charles became acutely aware of his biblical ignorance. The writers he studied often quoted passages from the Bible. In particular, these writers referred to Moses, the Old Testament Lawgiver. So Charles bought a Bible and began studying it. His analytical, inquiring mind caused him to be earnest in his studies, and he found himself intrigued with the Scriptures.

When a new minister, the Reverend George Gale, was called to the local Presbyterian church, Charles began attending church. Then, because of his love of music, he soon became choir director and had to be in church on a regular basis. For the first time in his twenty-nine years, he began to pay close attention to a minister's sermons.

Charles noted that the "Reverend Gale's preaching was of the old school type; that is, it was thoroughly

Calvinistic. I was not able to gain very much instruction from his preaching. As I sometimes told him, he seemed to me to begin in the middle of his discourse, and to assume many things which to my mind, needed to be proved." Charles believed, too, that "he seemed to take it for granted that his hearers were theologians, and therefore that he might assume all the great and fundamental doctrines of the gospel. But I was rather perplexed than edified by his preaching."

The sermons were scholarly and wooden, and Charles had difficulty following them. Gale's theology seemed illogical to Charles, and he told him so. To Charles's delight, the pastor often came by Benjamin Wright's law office on Mondays to discuss the previous day's sermon with Charles—even though Charles was often harsh and sometimes ungracious in his criticism.

Reverend Gale seemed anxious to know what impressions his sermons had made on the young lawyer. With complete honesty, Charles remarked that "I used to converse with him freely; and I now think I criticized his sermons unmercifully. I raised such objections against his positions as forced themselves upon my attention." One of the terms Charles wondered about was repentance. What did Gale mean by repentance? Was it a mere feeling of sorrow for sin? Was it altogether a passive state of mind, or did it involve a voluntary element? If it was a change of mind, in what respect was it a change of mind?

He also questioned Gale about the term regeneration. What did he mean by that word? What did such language mean when applied to a spiritual change? And what did Gale mean by faith? Was it merely an intellectual state?

Was it simply a conviction or persuasion that the things stated in the Gospels were true? Charles also queried Gale about the term sanctification. Did it involve any physical change in the subject, or any physical influence on the part of God? Charles pondered the deep meaning of each of these words—and others beside.

As a result of his questioning the Reverend Gale, Charles reported that "we had a great many interesting conversations; but they seemed rather to stimulate my own mind to inquiry, than to satisfy me in respect to the truth."

Instead of having his questions answered, Charles began to notice a growing restlessness within himself. The more he read the Bible and attended prayer meeting, the more anxious he became. As he realized, "A little consideration convinced me that I was by no means in a state of mind to go to heaven if I should die. It seemed to me that there must be something in religion that was of infinite importance; and it was soon settled with me, that if the soul was immortal, I needed a great change in my inward state to be prepared for happiness in heaven. But still my mind was not made up as to the truth or falsehood of the gospel and of the Christian religion. The question, however, was of too much importance to allow me to rest in any uncertainty on the subject."

Prayer was another aspect of the church that concerned Charles. He was particularly struck with the fact that the prayers he listened to from week to week were not, as far as he could tell, answered. In fact, he noted, "I understood from their utterances in prayer, and from other remarks in their meetings, that those who offered them did not regard them as answered."

He knew some of the Bible's promises by that time—especially what Christ said regarding prayer. He was puzzled about straightforward New Testament promises such as, "Ask, and it shall be given you; seek, and ye shall find; knock, and it shall be opened unto you: For every one that asketh receiveth; and he that seeketh findeth; and to him that knocketh it shall be opened" (Matthew 7:7–8). Why did not God answer prayers such as this one, if a person prayed in faith?

Another facet of prayer that was perplexing to Charles was that of asking for the Holy Spirit. He knew that Christ declared that He was more willing to give the Holy Spirit than parents were willing to give good gifts to their children. But why, when the people prayed continually for the outpouring of the Holy Spirit, did they not receive what they asked?

Charles also noticed that "they exhorted each other to wake up and be engaged, and to pray earnestly for a revival of religion, asserting that if they did their duty, prayed for the outpouring of the spirit, and were in earnest, that the spirit of God would be poured out, that they would have a revival of religion, and that the impenitent would be converted. But in their prayer and conference meetings they would continually confess substantially, that they were making no progress in securing a revival of religion."

Such inconsistency in people's prayers weighed on him. He puzzled over these people either not being true Christians and therefore not prevailing with God; or perhaps he misunderstood the promises and biblical teachings on the subject of prayer. Then again, maybe the

Bible was not true. These inconsistencies "almost drove me into skepticism," Charles noted, since "the teachings of the Bible did not at all accord with the facts which were before my eyes."

At one prayer meeting when asked if he desired people to pray for him, he refused, stating, "No. Because I do not see that God answers your prayers." He added: "I suppose I need to be prayed for, for I am conscious that I am a sinner; but I do not see that it will do any good for you to pray for me; for you are continually asking, but you do not receive. You have been praying for a revival of religion ever since I have been in Adams, and yet you have it not. You have been praying for the Holy Spirit to descend upon yourselves, and yet complaining of your leanness. You have prayed enough since I have attended these meetings to have prayed the devil out of Adams, if there is any virtue in your prayers. But here you are praying on, and complaining still." Charles's questioning continued seemingly without any answers.

As he looked more closely at the Scriptures, however, he wondered if the people failed to meet the conditions for prayer. Their prayers, it seemed to him, were not being prayed in faith. After struggling with this situation for years, he finally concluded that in spite of whatever he didn't understand, or the people or the pastor didn't understand, the Bible was the true Word of God.

Once he grasped this fact, Charles "was brought face to face with the question whether I would accept Christ as presented in the gospel, or pursue a worldly course of life. At this period, my mind, as I have since known, was so much impressed by the Holy Spirit, that I could not long leave this question unsettled; nor could I long hesitate between the two courses of life presented to me." Whatever decision he reached, Charles knew that the consequences would last for time and eternity.

four

Charles's search for the truth about the gospel was not hard to understand given the times he lived in. The religious scene in America had changed considerably since the arrival of the early Puritans in the 1600s.

The orthodox faith of the Puritans had been replaced in many quarters by Unitarianism, a belief system which questioned the deity of Christ, the nature of the Trinity, and the depravity of man, among other things. By the beginning of the 1800s, King's Chapel, the first Episcopalian church in Boston, had defected completely to the Unitarian fold. James Freeman, its pastor, preached persuasively on such themes as the divinity of Christ, the depravity of man, and the nature of the atonement, but he used unorthodox definitions for these terms. "There is one God," he insisted. But Christ was not God, Freeman taught. Christ came only to reveal God's nature.

Standard orthodox beliefs were held by people such as President Timothy Dwight of Yale, in New Haven, Connecticut. Although Yale had also been infiltrated by heresies such as deism and ideas from the French Enlightenment following the French Revolution, Dwight insisted on sound orthodox doctrine. When he became president of the school in 1785, he preached from an orthodox viewpoint, and revival broke out in 1800. That same year, a frontier awakening shook Kentucky, and the Holy Spirit began to stir other areas of the young nation as well.

Another New England divinity school, Harvard College, did not share in the religious awakening. Its professor of divinity, Henry Ware, came to Harvard in 1805 and persuaded many of the students to believe in Unitarianism. Another Unitarian, Noah Worchester, published a newspaper called *Bible News,* in which he set forth Unitarian beliefs.

In 1819, William Ellery Channing, a popular and influential Boston pastor, declared in his ordination message that the divinity of Christ was an illogical doctrine. Further, he rejected the idea of the depravity of man. Channing also preached that Christ's Passion accomplished little more than moral or spiritual deliverance through instruction, example, and death. He was not convinced that Christ's death paid the penalty for sin.

Another belief prevalent in New England at that time was Universalism. One Universalist preacher, the Reverend John Murray, stated in 1770 that "Christ's righteousness is upon all his seed; by his simple act many are made righteous." Murray believed that salvation was universal—

that is, because of Christ's death, everyone was redeemed, regardless of his or her own beliefs.

Murray organized the First Universalist Church in Gloucester, Massachusetts, in 1779. Just a few years later, the Reverend Charles Chauncy, pastor of the First Congregational Church of Boston, preached a sermon on the theme, "Salvation of all men." Then in 1785 enough Universalist congregations existed to justify holding a convention. In time, Unitarianism and Universalism began to merge.

Another movement that was in its formative stages by 1820 was transcendentalism. Deism was losing popularity because it was too impersonal for most people. Transcendentalism filled that void. Transcendentalists believed that nature was divine, the intimate god who is with us. The movement reached its height in the mid-nineteenth century and is expressed in the writings of Ralph Waldo Emerson and Henry David Thoreau.

However, thoughtful orthodox congregations existed as well. Their pastors followed in the tradition of Jonathan Edwards (1703–1758) and Samuel Hopkins (1721–1803). Charles Finney's pastor, the Reverend George Gale, proved to be staunchly orthodox. Fresh from Princeton, he was determined to promote the tenets of Calvinism. Gale emphasized, in particular, John Calvin's views on predestination and the Trinity. However, Gale tended to get too technical in his sermons, which meant not many conversions were taking place.

At one point during this time, Charles attended an inquiry meeting on salvation. He came under conviction and, as he said, "trembled so that my very seat shook under me." He admitted, too, that "I never received such instruction as I needed. For if I had, I should have been converted at once." Of course, the prayer meetings also hindered Finney's finding real faith. As he said, the people's prayers seemed to go nowhere. They were lifeless and futile.

Eventually Pastor Gale gave up on Finney. He advised the young people, "Don't pray for Charles Finney. He's too critical ever to find salvation." Gale believed that Charles had sinned against "so much light he is incapable of receiving the grace of God." Even Charles's influence on the choir he directed, according to Gale, would prevent the choir members from finding salvation. Nevertheless, many faithful believers continued to pray for Charles, including Lydia Root Andrews, a young lady from Whitestown, New York.

Despite the hindrances to Charles's ever obtaining salvation, he was favorably impressed by Gale and the church ministry—more so than the minister could have imagined. As Charles later admitted, "At Adams, for the first time, I sat regularly for a length of time, under an educated ministry."

In the summer of 1821, Pastor Gale took a trip to visit a sick sister. He left his pulpit to Jedediah Burchard with the instructions to do no more than read sermons from a book and give some exhortation. However, the Holy Spirit began to move the congregation, and Finney sensed that a revival was beginning in Adams. When Charles heard a man praying one day in a schoolhouse as he returned from a legal appointment, he became uneasy.

"That praying did more to impress my mind with the

subject of religion, than all I had heard before," he later reflected.

He became increasingly disturbed about his condition. He began asking himself some serious questions. In spite of the sermons not being logical to him, was there truth in what Pastor Gale preached? Were the church members' prayers really sincere? Even though the church people's prayers went largely unanswered, was there validity in their prayers? What about the Bible itself? Was it really the truth? Finally, he asked, "Does a person actually need a personal experience of Jesus Christ more than anything on earth? What must one do to be a genuine Christian?"

These were questions Charles had to ask. He had asked the people around him about their faith; now the tables were turned. It was up to him to answer his own questions. As Charles faced his questions squarely, the truth of the gospel began to break in upon him.

Charles recounted in later years the remarkable events which followed swiftly as the light of the gospel broke upon him:

> On a sabbath evening in the autumn of 1821, I made up my mind that I would settle the question of my soul's salvation at once, that if it were possible I would make my peace with God. But as I was very busy in the affairs of the office, I knew that without great firmness of purpose, I would never effectually attend to the subject. I therefore, then and there resolved, as far as possible, to avoid all business, and everything that would divert my attention, and to give myself wholly to

the work of securing the salvation of my soul. I carried this resolution into execution as sternly and thoroughly as I could. I was, however, obliged to be a good deal in the office. But as the providence of God would have it, I was not much occupied either on Monday or Tuesday; and had opportunity to read my Bible and engage in prayer most of the time.

But I was very proud without knowing it. I had supposed that I had not much regard for the opinions of others, whether they thought this or that in regard to myself; and I had in fact been quite singular in attending prayer meetings, and in the degree of attention that I had paid to religion, while in Adams. In this respect, I had been so singular as to leave the church at times to think that I must be an anxious inquirer. But I found, when I came to face the question, that I was very unwilling to have anyone know that I was seeking the salvation of my soul. When I prayed, I would only whisper my prayer, after having stopped the keyhole to the door, lest someone should discover that I was engaged in prayer. Before that time I had my Bible lying on the table with the law books; and it never had occurred to me to be ashamed of being found reading it, any more that I should be ashamed of being found reading any other of my books.

But after I had addressed myself in earnest to the subject of my own salvation, I kept my Bible, as much as I could, out of sight. If I was reading *it when anyone came in, I would throw my law books upon it, to create the impression that I had not had it in my hand. Instead of being outspoken and willing to talk with anyone and everybody on the subject as before, I found myself unwilling to converse with anybody. I did not want to see my minister, because I did not want to let him know how I felt, and I had no confidence that he would understand my case, and give me the direction that I needed. For the same reasons I avoided conversation with the elders of the church, or with any of the Christian people. I was ashamed to let them know how I felt, on the one hand; and on the other, I was afraid they would misdirect me. I felt myself shut up to the Bible.*

During Monday and Tuesday my conviction increased; but still it seemed as if my heart grew harder. I could not shed a tear; I could not pray. I had no opportunity to pray above my breath; and frequently I felt, that if I could be alone where I could use my voice and let myself out, I should find relief in prayer. I was shy, and avoided, as much as I could, speaking to anybody on any subject. I endeavored, however, to do this in a way that would excite no suspicion, in my mind, that I was seeking the salvation of my soul.

Tuesday night I had become very nervous; and in the night a strange feeling came over me as if I were about to die. I knew that if I did I should sink down to hell and felt almost like screaming; nevertheless, I quieted myself as best

I could until morning.

At an early hour I started for the office. But just before I arrived at the office, something seemed to confront me with questions like these: indeed, it seemed as if the inquiry was within myself as if an inward voice said to me, "What are you waiting for? Did you not promise to give your heart to God? And what are you trying to do? Are you en-deavoring to work out a right-eousness of your own?"

Just at that point the whole question of God's salvation opened to my mind in a manner most marvellous to me at that time. I think I saw then, as clearly as I ever had in my life, the reality and fullness of the atonement of Christ. I saw that His work was a finished work; that instead of having, or needing, any righteousness of my own to rec-ommend me to God, I had to submit myself to the righteousness of God through Christ. It was full and complete; and all that was necessary on my part was to get my own consent to give up my sins, and accept Christ. Salvation, it seemed to me, instead of being a thing to be wrought out, by one's own works, was a thing to be found entirely in the Lord Jesus Christ, who presented Himself before me as my God and my Savior.

Without being distinctly aware of it, I had stopped in the street right where the inward voice seemed to arrest me. How long I remained in that position I cannot say, but after this distinct reve-lation had stood for some little time before my mind, the question seemed to be put, "Will you accept it now, today?" I replied, "Yes; I will accept today, or I will die in the attempt."

North of the village inn, and over a hill, lay a grove of woods, in which I was in the almost daily habit of walking, more or less, when it was pleasant weather. It was now October, and the time was past for my frequent walks there. Nevertheless, instead of going to my office, I turned and bent my course towards the woods, feeling that I must be alone, and away from all human eyes and ears, so that I could pour out my prayer to God.

But still my pride must show itself. As I went over the hill, it occurred to me that someone might see me and suppose that I was going away to pray. Yet, probably there was not a person on earth that would have suspected such a thing, had he seen me going. But so great was my pride, and so much was I possessed with the fear of man, that I recollect that I skulked along under the fence till I got so far out of sight that no one from the village could see me. I then penetrated into the woods. I should think, a quarter of a mile, went over to the other side of the hill, and found a place where some large trees had fallen across each other, leaving an open place between. There I saw I could make a kind of closet. I crept into this place and knelt down for prayer. As I turned to go up into the woods, I recollect to have said, "I will give my heart to God, or I will never come *down from there." I recollect repeating this as I went up—"I will give my heart to God before I ever come down again."*

But when I attempted to pray I found that my heart could not pray. I had supposed that if I could only be where I could speak aloud, without being overheard, I could pray freely. But lo! when I came to try, I was dumb; that is, I had nothing to say to God; or at least I could say but a few words, and those without heart. In attempting to pray I would hear a rustling in the leaves, as I thought, and would stop and look up to see if someone were not coming. This I did several times.

Finally I found myself verging fast to despair. I said to myself, "I cannot pray. My heart is dead to God, and I will not pray." I then reproached myself for having promised to give my heart to God before I left the woods. When I came to try, I found I could not give my heart to God. My inward soul hung back, and there was no going out of my heart to God. I began to feel deeply that it was too late; that it must be that I was given up of God and was passed over.

As Charles struggled with these dismal thoughts, he was in considerable anguish. He mulled over ideas about God and salvation, the way of salvation, and conviction of sin over and over in his mind. How much he wanted to be free from guilt and condemnation! He could only hope he was near the end of his quest.

five

S till waiting to hear from God, Charles continued
kneeling in the wooded area. His anxieties nearly
overwhelmed him. He felt as though he was being
bombarded by confusion:

*The thought was pressing me of the rashness of
my promise, that I would give my heart to God
that day or die in the attempt. It seemed to me as
if that were binding upon my soul; and yet I was
not going to break my vow. A great sinking and
discouragement came over me, and I felt almost
too weak to stand upon my knees. Just at this
moment I again thought I heard someone
approach me, and I opened my eyes to see
whether it were so. But right there the revelation
of my pride of heart, and the great difficulty that
stood in the way, was distinctly shown to me. An*

overwhelming sense of my wickedness in being ashamed to have a human being see me on my knees before God took such powerful possession of me that I cried at the top of my voice, and exclaimed that I would not leave the place if all the men on earth and all the devils in hell surrounded me. "What!" I said, "such a de-graded sinner as I am, on my knees confessing my sins to the great and holy God; and ashamed to have any human being, and a sinner like myself, find me on my knees endeavoring to make peace with my offended God!" The sin appeared awful, infinite. It broke me down before the Lord.

Just at that point this passage of Scripture seemed to drop into my mind with a flood of light: "Then shall ye go and pray unto Me, and find Me, when ye shall search for Me with all your heart." I instantly seized hold of this with my heart. I had intellectually believed the Bible before; but never had truth been in my mind that faith was a voluntary trust instead of an intellectual state. I was as conscious as I was of my existence, of trusting at that moment in God's veracity. Somehow I knew that that was a passage of Scripture, though I do not think I had ever read it. I knew that it was God's word, and God's voice, as it were, that spoke to me. I cried to Him, "Lord, I take Thee at Thy word. Now Thou knowest that I do search for Thee with all my heart, and that I have come here to pray to Thee; and Thou hast promised to hear me."

That seemed to settle the question that I could then, that day perform my vow. The Spirit seemed to lay stress upon that idea in the text. "When you search for Me with all your heart." The question of when, that is, of the present time, seemed to fall heavily into my heart. I told the Lord that I should take Him at His word: that He could not lie, and that therefore I was sure that He heard my prayer, and that He would be found of me.

He then gave me many other promises, both from the Old and the New Testament, especially some most precious promises respecting our Lord Jesus Christ. I never can, in words, make any human being understand how precious and true those promises appeared to me. I took them one after the other as infallible truth, the assertions of God who could not lie. They did not seem so much to fall into my intellect as into my heart; to be put within the grasp of the voluntary powers of my mind; and I seized hold of them, appropriated them, and fastened upon them with the grasp of a drowning man.

I continued thus to pray, and to receive and appropriate promises for a long time. I know not how long. I prayed till my mind became so full that, before I was aware of it, I was on my feet, tripping up the ascent toward the road. The question of my being converted had not so much as arisen in my thought; but as I went up, rushing through the leaves and bushes, I recollect saying with great emphasis, "If I am ever converted, I will preach the gospel."

I soon reached the road that led to the village, and began to reflect upon what had passed; I found that my mind had become most wonderfully quiet and peaceful. I said to myself, "What is this? I must have grieved the Holy Ghost entirely away. I have lost all my conviction. I have not a particle of concern about my soul; and it must be that the Spirit has left me. Why!" thought I, "I never was so far from being concerned about my own salvation in my life."

Then I remembered what I had said to God while I was on my knees—that I had said that I would take Him at His word; and indeed I recollected a good many things that I had said, and concluded that it was no wonder that the Spirit had left me; that for such a sinner as I was to take hold of God's word in that way, was presumption if not blasphemy. I concluded that in my excitement I had grieved the Holy Spirit, and perhaps committed the unpardonable sin.

I walked quietly toward the village; and so perfectly quiet was my mind that it seemed as if all nature listened. It was on the 10th of October, and a very pleasant day. I had gone into the woods immediately after early daybreak; and when I returned to the village I found it was dinner time. Yet I had been wholly unconscious of the time that had passed; it appeared to me that I had gone from the village but a short time.

But how was I to account for the quiet in the

*mind? I tried to recall my convictions, to get back
again the load of sin under which I was laboring.
But all sense of sin, all consciousness of present
sin or guilt, had departed from me. I said to
myself, "What is this, that I cannot arouse any
sense of guilt in my soul, as great a sinner as I
am?" I tried in vain to make myself anxious
about my present state. I was so quiet and peaceful that I tried to feel concerned about that, lest it
should be a result of my having grieved the Spirit
away. But take any view of it I would, I could not
be anxious at all about my soul, and about my
spiritual state. The repose of my mind was
unspeakably great. I never can describe it in
words. The thought of God was sweet to my mind,
and the most profound spiritual tranquillity had
taken full possession of me.*

Charles's questions about the gospel were gone. In their
place, he sensed a new peace, joy, and tranquillity. He
could scarcely take in the great peace that flooded his life.
Charles remembered the profoundness of his conversion
and its aftermath in these words:

*I went to my dinner, and found I had no appetite
to eat. I then went to the office, and found that
Squire Wright had gone to dinner. I took down my
bass-viol, and, as I was accustomed to do, began
to play and sing some pieces of sacred music. But
as soon as I began to sing those sacred words, I
began to weep. It seemed as if my heart was all*

liquid; and my feelings were in such a state that I could not hear my own voice in singing without causing my sensibility to overflow. I wondered of this, and tried to suppress my tears, but could not. After trying in vain to suppress my tears, I put up my instrument and stopped singing.

After dinner we were engaged in removing our books and furniture to another office. We were very busy in this, and had but little conversation all the afternoon. My mind, however, remained in that profoundly tranquil state. There was a great sweetness and tenderness in my thoughts and soul. Everything appeared to be going right, and nothing seemed to ruffle or disturb me in the least.

Just before evening the thought took possession of my mind, that as soon as I was left alone in the new office, I would try to pray again—that I was not going to abandon the subject of religion and give it up, at any rate; and therefore, although I no longer had any concern about my soul, still I would continue to pray.

By evening we got the books and furniture adjusted; and I made up, in an open fireplace, a good fire, hoping to spend the evening alone. Just at dark Squire Wright, seeing that everything was adjusted, bade me good-night and went to his home. I had accompanied him to the door; and as I closed the door and turned around, my heart seemed to be liquid within me. All my feelings seemed to rise and flow out; and *the utterance of my heart was, "I want to pour my whole soul out to God." The rising of my soul was so great that I rushed into the room back of the front office, to pray. There was no fire, and no light, in the room; nevertheless, it appeared to me as if it were perfectly light. As I went in and shut the door after me, it seemed to me that I saw Him as I would see any other man. He said nothing, but looked at me in such a manner as to break me right down at His feet. I have always since regarded this as a most remarkable state of mind; for it seemed to me a reality, that He stood before me, and I fell down at His feet and poured out my soul to Him. I wept aloud like a child, and made such confessions as I could with my choked utterance. It seemed to me that I bathed His feet with my tears; and yet I had no distinct impression that I touched Him, that I recollect.*

I must have continued in this state for a good while; but my mind was too much absorbed with the interview to recollect anything that I said. But I know, as soon as my mind became calm enough to break off from the interview, I returned to the front office, and found that the fire that I had made of large wood was nearly burned out. But as I turned and was about to take a seat by the fire, I received a mighty baptism of the Holy Ghost. Without any expectation of it, without ever having the thought in my mind that there was any such thing for me, without my recollection that I had ever heard the thing mentioned by any person in the world, the Holy Spirit descended upon me in a manner that seemed to go through me, body and soul. I could feel the impression, like a wave of electricity, going through and through me. Indeed, it seemed to come in waves and waves of liquid love; for I could not express it in any other way. And yet it did not seem like water but rather the breath of God. I can recollect distinctly that it seemed to fan me, like immense wings; and it seemed to me, as these waves passed over me, that they literally moved my hair like a passing breeze.

No words can express the wonderful love that was shed abroad in my heart. I wept aloud with joy and love; and I do not know but I should say, I literally bellowed out the unutterable gushings of my heart. These waves came over me, and over me, and over me, one after another, until I recollect I cried out, "I shall die if these waves continue to pass over me." I said, "Lord, I cannot bear any more": yet I had no fear of death.

How long I continued in this state, with this baptism continuing to roll over me and go through me, I do not know. But I know it was late in the evening when a member of my choir—for I was the leader of the choir—came into the office to see me. He was a member of the church. He found me in this state of loud weeping, and said to me, "Mr. Finney, what ails you?" I could make him no answer at that time.

Then he said, "Are you in pain?" I gathered myself up as best I could, and replied, "No, but so happy that I cannot live."

He turned and left the office. And in a few minutes returned with one of the elders of the church, whose shop was nearly across the way from our office. This elder was a very serious man; and in my presence had been very watchful, and I had scarcely ever seen him laugh. When he came in, I was very much in the state in which I was when the young man went out to call him. He asked me how I felt, and I began to tell him. Instead of saying anything, he fell into a spasmodic laughter. It seemed as if it was impossible for him to keep from laughing from the very bottom of his heart.

There was a young man in the neighborhood who was preparing for college, with whom I had been very intimate. Our minister, as I afterward learned, had repeatedly talked with him on the subject of religion, and warned him against being misled by me. He informed him that I was a very careless young man about religion; and he thought that if he associated much with me his mind would be diverted, and he would not be converted.

After I was converted, and this young man was converted, he told me that he had said to Mr. Gale several times, when he had admonished him about associating so much with me, that my conversations had often affected him more, *religiously, than his preaching. I had, indeed, let out my feelings a good deal to this young man.*

But just at the time when I was giving an account of my feelings to this elder of the church, and to another member who was with him, this young man came into the office. I was sitting with my back towards the door, and barely observed that he came in. He listened with astonishment to what I was saying, and the first I knew he partly fell upon the floor, and cried out in the greatest agony of mind, "Do pray for me!" The elder of the church and the other member knelt down and began to pray for him; and when they had prayed, I prayed for him myself. Soon after this they all retired and left me alone.

The question then arose in my mind, "Why did Elder B. laugh so? Did he not think that I was under a delusion, or crazy?" This suggestion brought a kind of darkness over my mind; and I began to query with myself whether it was proper for me—such a sinner as I had been—to pray for that young man. A cloud seemed to shut in over me; I had no hold upon anything in which I could rest; and after a little while I retired to bed, not distressed in mind, but still at a loss to know what to make of my present state. Notwithstanding the baptism I had received, this temptation so obscured my view that I went to bed without feeling sure that my peace was made with God.

I soon fell asleep, but almost as soon awoke again on account of the great flow of the love of

*God that was in my heart. I was so filled with
love that I could not sleep. Soon I fell asleep
again, and awoke in the same manner. When
I awoke, this temptation would return upon me,
and the love that seemed to be in my heart
would abate; but as soon as I was asleep, it was
so warm within me that I would immediately
awake. This continued till, late at night, I
obtained sound repose. When I awoke in the
morning the sun had risen and was pouring a
clear light into my room. Words cannot express
the impression that this sunlight made upon me.
Instantly the baptism that I had received the
night before returned upon me in the same manner. I arose upon my knees in the bed, and wept
aloud with joy, and remained for some time too
much overwhelmed with the baptism of the
Spirit to do anything but pour out my soul to
God. It seemed as if this morning's baptism was
accompanied with a gentle reproof, and the
Spirit seemed to say to me, "Will you doubt?"
"Will you doubt?" I cried, "No! I will not
doubt; I cannot doubt." He then cleared the subject up so much to my mind that it was in fact
impossible for me to doubt that the Spirit of
God had taken possession of my soul.*

Charles tried to pull himself together. The dynamic experience he had just had had washed away every last vestige
of doubt and questioning. Immediately, he went to the
law office where he told Squire Benjamin Wright what

45

God had just done in his life. Astounded, the judge just looked at Charles with a fixed stare but said nothing. God was also at work in the judge, bringing him to a point of conviction.

Then a client, who was also a deacon in the church, came into the office. Charles was scheduled to try a case in court for him that very day. The man asked him, "Mr. Finney, do you recollect that my case is to be tried at ten this morning? I suppose you are ready?"

Charles responded, "Deacon, I have a retainer from the Lord Jesus Christ to plead His cause, and I cannot plead yours."

The deacon looked at Charles in amazement, and asked, "What do you mean?"

So Charles replied that he had enlisted in the cause of Christ and he must only plead the cause of Christ. The man lowered his head without saying a word and left the office. But Charles's simple testimony marked the deacon, and before long, he had experienced a wonderful renewal in his life.

Charles did not hesitate after that. Christ became his consuming passion, and to all who would listen, he shared the love of Christ. God had wondrously touched his life and changed him, and he wanted everyone he met to know this great truth. No longer could he be interested in pursuing his career in law.

As he began to share Christ, Charles became aware that after just a few words to someone, the person would come under conviction. Every word he spoke seemed accompanied by the power of the Holy Spirit. Soon, people were being saved all over the town of Adams. Everyone in the small town was talking about what had happened to Charles Finney. His conversion might just as well have made bold headlines in the town newspaper.

When the Reverend George Gale returned from his visit to his sister, he was probably the most shocked over Charles's conversion. Pastor Gale usually held prayer meetings in the school building. One evening after his return, even though no meeting was scheduled, the school building filled up with people. Everyone sat quietly with rapt attention. Finally, since no one stood up to take charge of the meeting, Charles exclaimed to himself, *My God, is it I?* Convinced that the Lord wanted him to, the new convert stood up to speak.

As Charles told the people about his dramatic experience with Christ, everyone in the room seemed struck with awe. Pastor Gale, especially, was moved by what God had done in Charles's life. To his credit, the pastor stood up and admitted to the congregation that he had doubted Charles's conversion until that night. He acknowledged that he had listened to a town skeptic who thought Charles was perpetrating a great hoax on the community. Now, the completely humbled pastor recognized God's power at work in Charles.

Almost at once, Charles sought to win the young people of Adams to Christ. He told the Reverend Gale, "For years I have led these young people astray. They have followed my example as an unconverted, skeptical pagan, now I want them to know that if Christ can transform my life, He can change them, too." He was gratified that many of the young people found salvation.

Many people from Adams were so impressed with Charles's experience that they sought out the same spot in the woods where he had knelt, hoping the Lord would meet them in a similar way. In fact, Judge Wright himself followed Charles's example by seeking the Lord in the woods. Before long, the whole community was caught up in a revival.

Charles realized he needed to visit his parents in Henderson, New York, and share his good news with them. When his father, whom Charles called "an unconverted man," greeted him at the gate with, "How do you do, Charles?" Charles replied, "I am well, father, body and soul. But, father, you are an old man; all your children are grown up and have left your house; and I never heard a prayer in my father's house."

After Charles said this to his father, the old man lowered his head and burst into tears, crying out, "I know it, Charles; come in and pray yourself!" It was not long before the entire Finney household came to Christ.

During the year after Charles's conversion, at least sixty-three people were converted in Adams and joined the Presbyterian church. The whole town seemed caught up in a fervency of prayer and revival. If Charles discovered any "cooling down" toward Christ, he would go to their homes to pray and counsel with them. During this time, Charles sensed an urgent need to pray. His practice was to go to church early every morning and intercede for the community. Other members soon joined him as they, too, sought the Lord.

In a little while, however, prayer meeting attendance

at the local churches began to wane. Deeply concerned, Charles cried out to God to continue His work in the community. One morning as he arrived at the church, Charles was startled to see the Reverend Gale already there. As he came to the door, Charles was suddenly overwhelmed by the glory of God shining around him.

Overcome by the great light, Charles noted, "All at once a light perfectly ineffable shone in my soul, that almost prostrated me to the ground. In this light it seemed as if I could see that all nature praised and worshipped God except man. This light seemed to be like the brightness of the sun in every direction. It was too intense for the eyes. I recollect casting my eyes down and breaking into a flood of tears, in view of the fact that mankind did not praise God. I think I knew something then, by actual experience, of that light that prostrated Paul on his way to Damascus. It was surely a light such as I could not have endured long."

Charles continued, "When I burst out into such loud weeping, Mr. Gale said, 'What is the matter, brother Finney?' I could not tell him. I found that he had seen no light; and that he saw no reason why I should be in such a state of mind. I therefore said but little. I believe I merely replied, that I saw the glory of God; and that I could not endure to think of the manner in which He was treated by men. Indeed, it did not seem to me at the time that the vision of His glory which I had, was to be described in words. I wept it out; and the vision, if it may be so called, passed away and left my mind calm."

Charles had frequent experiences like this in the years immediately after his conversion. Although at times he tried to relate them to others, he found that his words fell on deaf ears. The Lord seemed to indicate that he was not to tell others about these unique experiences.

Charles practically "prayed without ceasing," as he said. He also had seasons of examining his soul. He later described these experiences with these words: "Sometimes I would pursue a wrong course in fasting, and attempt to examine myself according to the ideas of self-examination then entertained by my minister and the church. I would try to look into my own heart, in the sense of examining my feelings; and would turn my attention particularly to my motives, and the state of my mind. When I pursued this course, I found invariably that the day would close without any perceptible advance being made."

He realized later why this happened: "Turning my attention, as I did, from the Lord Jesus Christ, and looking into myself, examining my motives and feelings, my feelings all subsided of course. But whenever I fasted, and let the Spirit take His own course with me, and gave myself up to let Him lead and instruct me, I universally found it in the highest degree useful. I found I could not live without enjoying the presence of God; and if at any time a cloud came over me, I could not rest, I could not study, I could not attend to anything with the least satisfaction or benefit, until the medium was again cleared between my soul and God."

Once his spiritual questions were settled, Charles found himself in another kind of dilemma. Although he had been very fond of his chosen profession of law, he realized that he no longer had much interest in practicing it. As he pondered what to do, he concluded that "I had no more any pleasure in attending to law business. I had many very pressing invitations to conduct lawsuits, but I uniformly refused. I did not dare trust myself in the excitement of a contested lawsuit; and furthermore, the business itself of conducting other people's controversies, appeared odious and offensive to me."

Meanwhile, Charles had entered into a rewarding life of prayer. He recounts one arresting experience he had at this time: "Not long after I was converted, a woman with whom I had boarded—though I did not board with her at this time—was taken very sick. She was not a Christian, but her husband was a professor of religion. He came into our office one evening, being a brother of Squire Wright, and said to me, 'My wife cannot live through the night.' This remark seemed to plant an arrow, as it were, in my heart. It came upon me in the sense of a burden that crushed me, the nature of which I could not at all understand; but with it an intense desire to pray for that woman. The burden was so great that I left my office almost immediately, and went up to the meeting house, to pray for her. There I struggled, but could not say much. I could only groan with groanings loud and deep.

"I stayed a considerable time in the church, in this state of mind, but got no relief. I returned to the office; but I could not sit still. I could only walk the room and agonize. I returned to the meeting house again, and went through the same process of struggling. For a long time I tried to get my prayer before the Lord; but somehow words could not express it. I could only groan and weep, without being able to express what I wanted in words. I

51

returned to the office again, and still found I was unable to rest; and I returned a third time to the meeting house. At this time the Lord gave me power to prevail. I was enabled to roll the burden upon Him; and I obtained the assurance in my own mind that the woman would not die, and indeed that she would never die in her sins."

When Charles returned to the office, his mind was quiet and peaceful, and he went home to rest. The next morning the woman's husband came to the office. Charles asked if his wife was doing any better, and the man replied smiling, "She's alive, and to all appearance better this morning."

Charles responded: "Brother, she will not die with this sickness; you may rely upon it. And she will never die in her sins." Charles was not certain how he understood this, but he had no doubt that it was true. Later the woman did in fact recover, and soon after, she came to faith in Christ.

Although Charles did not fully understand that prayer experience, when he later shared with another Christian what had happened to him, the man explained, "Why, that was the travail of your soul." As the two talked further, the man pointed him to Scripture passages and helped Charles to better understand the experience.

Another experience Charles had with prayer concerned a young woman in his community. Many of the other Christians in the vicinity knew she was not converted, although they acknowledged that she was intelligent, charming, and knew much about religion. This being the case, Charles and one of the elders of the church agreed to pray for her daily—in fact, they agreed to pray three times a day: morning, noon, and night.

Much to Charles's dismay, however, after the two had prayed for some time, he realized the elder was losing his desire to pray for her. Charles continued to pray unabated. Then one evening he went to the woman's house, and as he neared the door, he heard scuffling and a female voice cry out. After several minutes, when the noise subsided, a woman opened the door. Charles noted that "she was pale and very much agitated. She held out that portion of the book which she had in her hand, and said, 'Mr. Finney, don't you think my sister has become a Universalist?' The book was a defense of Universalism. Her sister had detected her reading it in a private way, and tried to get it away from her; and it was the struggle to obtain that book which I had heard."

Upon hearing this news, Charles declined to go in. The news he had just received, as he said, "Struck me very much in the same way as had the announcement that the sick woman, already mentioned, was about to die. It loaded me down with great agony. As I returned to my room, at some distance from that house, I felt almost as if I should stagger under the burden that was on my mind; and I struggled, and groaned, and agonized, but could not frame to present the case before God in words, but only in groans and tears.

"It seemed to me that the discovery that that young woman, instead of being converted, was becoming a Universalist, so astounded me that I could not break through with my faith, and get hold of God in reference to her case. There seemed to be a darkness hanging over the question, as if a cloud had risen up between me and God, in regard to prevailing for her salvation. But still the Spirit struggled within me with groanings that could not be uttered."

When Charles went to bed that evening, he sensed he had not prevailed in prayer for the young woman. However, he noted that "as soon as it was light I awoke; and the first thought that I had was to beseech the God of grace again for that young woman. I immediately arose and fell upon my knees. No sooner was I upon my knees than the darkness gave way, and the whole subject opened to my mind; and as soon as I plead for her God said to me, 'Yes! yes!' If He had spoken with an audible voice, it would not have been more distinctly understood than was this word spoken within my soul. It instantly relieved all my solicitude. My mind became filled with the greatest peace and joy; and I felt a complete certainty that her salvation was secure." The woman was converted sometime later, although not immediately, as had happened in the earlier case.

Charles had many wonderful adventures in prayer at that time, but sometimes God said no to Charles's requests. One time when he had earnestly cried out to God for a certain magistrate's salvation, the man came under conviction for his sins. However, day after day, he kept putting off actually becoming a Christian. In prayer, the Lord admonished Charles with "No; I will not hear." It seemed to Charles that the Lord told him not to pray any more about the man.

Charles saw the man the following morning and reminded him that he needed to commit his life to God. The man replied indignantly, "Mr. Finney, I shall have nothing more to do with it until I return from the legislature. I stand committed to my political friends to carry out certain measures in the legislature, that are incompatible with my first becoming a Christian; and I have promised that I will not attend to the subject until after I have returned from Albany."

When the magistrate revealed his thoughts to Charles, Charles could better understand why the Lord had given him no for an answer. Over time, the man traveled farther away from God and, at the end, rejected Him completely.

Charles realized he was totally caught up in sharing the gospel of Christ. He decided to turn from the law and seek to become a minister.

six

When Charles began to prepare for the ministry, he recalled how eagerly he had studied law. Now he had been called by the Lord Himself—as Charles saw it, a "retainer" from the Lord of the universe to be Christ's advocate, a minister of the gospel. He entered this new field of study with even more vigor than he had the law.

In the Presbyterian church, a young man called to preach came under the care of a presbytery—a ruling group of elders and ministers within the church. When the presbytery urged Charles in 1823 to attend Princeton Theological Seminary, he balked. The ministers asked Charles why he would not go to Princeton, and he told them that his views on religion differed from those of the seminary. Further, he admitted that "I would not put myself under such an influence as they had been under; that I was confident they had been wrongly educated, and they were not ministers that met my ideal of what a minister of Christ should be. I told them this reluctantly, but I could not honestly withhold it."

In the nineteenth century, Princeton Theological Seminary represented what was then called "old school Calvinistic theology." Early on, the seminary had reaped many benefits from the influence of a revival known as the First Great Awakening. In fact, Jonathan Edwards, revivalist, educator, and Calvinist, had served as president of Princeton at one time.

Needless to say, Charles's decision not to attend Princeton shook the staid ministers who made up his presbytery. They wondered how he could ever be a successful minister of the gospel without formal training. But Charles was far more prepared than he or the ministers realized. His legal training had given him expertise in logic, rhetoric, argumentation, ethics, and the power of analysis.

Even his impressive physical appearance and handsome frame were instruments to be used by God in Charles's preaching. His voice, too, possessed a clear, resonant quality that pleased the ears of his listeners. His personal style, while not preachy, employed not only the Bible, but Shakespeare and Blackstone as well.

Someone has said of Charles's power as he preached that "the hearer never felt, till the close, that he was listening to a sermon, but rather that he was being personally addressed with much earnestness upon matters that were of great mutual concern." Another person observed that Charles's words were "logic on fire," crashing through his listeners "like cannonballs through a basket of eggs."

Many of Charles's contemporaries no doubt would have agreed with his decision not to attend Princeton and follow a theological course. They could perhaps see that such rigid schooling would have done him more harm than good.

So the presbytery agreed on June 25, 1823, to place Charles under the tutelage of the Reverend George W. Gale and the Reverend George Boardman, pastor of the Presbyterian church in Watertown, New York. Both of these tutors were steeped in the truths of Princeton Calvinism. Charles welcomed the designation. He knew he needed training and was more than willing to submit to these older ministers in the hopes of becoming a full-fledged minister himself.

However, Charles continued to find much fault with Pastor Gale's Calvinism. When Gale preached on repentance, he would remind his congregation that they could not repent unless God granted them the will to do so. He would also demand that his hearers have faith. There again, he believed that one could not have faith unless he was of the elect. Charles could not understand the reasoning behind these teachings and refused to go along with them.

Actually Charles found himself puzzled by much of Gale's "old school" theology. To the young ministerial student, Gale's theology was not logical. In addition, he found it impossible to justify this style of Calvinism from a scriptural standpoint. Overall, Charles could not find Gale's (and the Calvinists') point of view in the Bible. Charles took matters into his own hands and began to build his theological base on "close and logical reasoning," according to his legal training.

Charles figured that the numerous conversions that resulted from his preaching were a sign that God honored his doctrinal views. On the other hand, Pastors Gale and Broadman could not claim many visible results from their preaching. His biggest objection to Pastor Gale's Calvinistic theology was his sense that Gale did not possess the power of the Holy Spirit in his ministry.

So the disputes between Gale and his pupil continued. Undoubtedly the sessions the two men had were interesting and lively, and, at one point, they intrigued even the congregation. Charles and Gale were in the midst of an absorbing session on the atonement when the church began to fill up for the service. When the two men started to break off their discussion, the people urged them to continue, fascinated by the arresting debate going on; so the discussion went on through what would have been the evening worship service.

Although Pastor Gale possessed a fine theological library which Charles used often as he sought answers to his questions, the volumes mostly approached issues from a Calvinistic viewpoint. This situation not only aggravated Charles, but was depressing to him as well. Charles struggled over the differences in his and Gale's positions on the atonement, regeneration, faith, repentance, the slavery of the will, and several similar doctrines. Gale, however, was insistent on his views; he sometimes became impatient with Charles because he differed with him on so many points.

The Reverend Gale misunderstood Charles's inquisitive turn of mind, labeling his disagreement on these major doctrines "reasoning." He cautioned him about becoming an infidel if he persisted in these doctrines and told him of Princeton students who had become infidels because they would not accept the confession of faith and the teaching of the doctors at the school. Mr. Gale also warned Charles that he would never be a useful minister unless he embraced the truth—that is, the truth as Gale believed it and taught it.

The situation between the two men reached such an impasse that Charles despaired of continuing his ministerial training. Charles knew in his heart he simply could not adhere to Pastor Gale's doctrines. One member of Gale's church, however, whom Charles knew to be "a very godly, praying man," began to pray with and for Charles. The man was an adherent of Calvinistic doctrine, but he was willing to listen to Charles and consider his views. Charles found comfort as the two "had frequent and protracted conversations," and "Elder H. became satisfied that I was right. He would call on me frequently to have seasons of prayer with me, to strengthen me in my studies, and in my discussions with Mr. G., and to decide me more and more firmly that, come what would, I would preach the Gospel."

After Charles got into the ministry and experienced great opposition to his preaching, he ran into Elder H. after a long absence. The man told him, "Oh! my soul is so burdened that I pray for you day and night. But I am sure that God will help. Go on, go on, brother Finney; the Lord will give you deliverance."

Despite the disagreements Charles had with the two ministers, all the discussions served to sharpen his debating

skills. Mr. Gale became ill after Charles had been studying theology for a few months, and a Universalist minister preached in his place, teaching that everyone would
go to heaven. Charles was distressed that "the impenitent
part of the community seemed very much disposed to
hear him, and finally people became so interested that
there was a large number that seemed to be shaken in their
minds, in regard to the commonly received views of the
Bible."

The situation was grievous to Mr. Gale and the church
elders, and they asked Charles if he would talk to the people about Universalism and see if he could refute the
man's arguments. Aware that the overall argument of the
Universalist was to show that sin did not deserve endless
punishment, Charles began to prepare himself for the
encounter. The Universalist pastor considered the doctrine of endless punishment as unjust, infinitely cruel,
and absurd. He would say, "God is love; how could a God
of love punish men endlessly?"

Charles made a startling announcement to the congregation one evening: "This Universalist preacher
holds forth doctrines that are new to me, and I do not
believe they are taught in the Bible. But I am going to
examine the subject, and if I cannot show that his views
are false, I will become a Universalist myself." Then
Charles set up a time when he would deliver a lecture
opposing the Universalist's views. Charles noticed, "the
Christian people were rather startled at my boldness in
saying that I would be a Universalist, if I could not prove
that his doctrines were false. However, I felt sure that I
could." Charles was able to refute the Universalist on the

doctrine of eternal punishment.

That was not the end of the discussions, however, because the man soon raised another issue: that of the atonement of Christ. In Pastor Gale's doctrine, the atonement of Christ was the literal payment of the debt of the elect, a suffering of just what they deserved to suffer. The elect were saved upon principles of exact justice. Christ, so far as they were concerned, had fully answered the demands of the law. All the Universalist had to do was to prove that the atonement was made for all men, and then he could show that all men would be saved because the debt of all mankind had been paid by the Lord Jesus Christ. Universalism would logically follow on the grounds of justice: God could not justly punish those whose debt was paid.

Again, Charles was called by the Reverend Gale and the elders to respond to the Universalist. Charles was willing to do so, but he had to confront Pastor Gale first. He told him, "Mr. Gale, I cannot do it without contradicting your views on that subject, and setting them all aside. With your views of the atonement he cannot be answered. For if you have the right view of the atonement, the people can easily see that the Bible proves that Christ died for all men, for the whole world of sinners; and therefore unless you will allow me to sweep your views of the atonement all away, I can say nothing to any purpose."

Mr. Gale recognized that Charles's position made some sense. He responded, "Well, it will never do to let the thing remain as it is. You may say what you please; only go on and answer him in your own way. If I find it necessary to preach on the subject of the atonement, I shall be obliged to contradict you."

Charles readily agreed. "Very well. Let me but show my views, and I can answer the Universalist; and you may say to the people afterward what you please."

Preparing for his presentation, Charles decided to use the Gospels to refute the Universalist's argument. While the Reverend Gale and other Calvinists agreed with the Universalist view up to a point, they reasoned that Christ died only for the elect, a position known as "limited atonement." Charles absolutely rejected such a view, believing that Christ died for the sins of all people.

So Charles began his debate by arguing that Christ's atonement was not a literal payment of the sinner's debt in any mathematical, legal sense. Instead, the Lord's death and resurrection merely did what was essential in God's sight to procure the forgiveness of sin and effect salvation. He urged that Christ's death on the cross satisfied what he termed "public justice," a phrase borrowed from Jonathan Edwards. This view of Christ's atoning work became central in Charles's theology. By taking this approach, Charles was convinced he had successfully defeated the Universalist position.

After he had studied with Pastors Gale and Boardman for six months, Charles came before the presbytery to be examined. As the men questioned him, he was asked if he believed in the Westminster Confession of Faith, a statement of beliefs held by Presbyterians. Charles replied that so far as he understood it, he believed it. Actually, he had never seen the document.

He was expected to deliver a sermon following the questioning, so in keeping with the tradition of his day, he had prepared his sermon by writing it out. As he began his delivery, he soon departed from the written pages and preached extemporaneously. Even though Charles failed to stick to his written sermon, his performance was deemed acceptable by the elders, and he was licensed to preach in the Presbyterian church.

The Sunday after he was licensed, Charles preached for the Reverend Gale. But when he came down from the pulpit, his pastor said to him, "Mr. Finney, I shall be very ashamed to have it known, wherever you go, that you studied theology with me." Although Charles was accustomed to Gale's disapproval, this remark hurt him deeply and discouraged him.

Later on, Pastor Gale asked Charles's forgiveness for his attitude toward him and wholeheartedly embraced Charles's theology. He told him then that he was glad Charles had not been influenced by his theology and doctrine.

As Charles struggled with what he believed were Pastor Gale's "erroneous doctrines," he became aware of another question the older man's ministry raised: If Pastor Gale had been converted to Christ, why had he never received the divine anointing of the Holy Spirit that would make him a power in the pulpit and in society for the conversion of souls?

The following summer, on July 1, 1824, the St. Lawrence Presbytery met at Evans Mills, New York, to ordain Charles. After calling the meeting to order and hearing a sermon given by the Reverend J. Clinton, the elders laid hands on Charles, and he became the Reverend Charles Grandison Finney, Presbyterian minister. When that October the Synod of Albany, New York, met in the First Presbyterian Church of Utica, Charles was present as a newly ordained Presbyterian minister.

The St. Lawrence Presbytery meeting proved to be important for Charles. In addition to his ordination, he met the Reverend Daniel Nash for the first time. Nash at one time had been spiritually cold, but during an illness, God did a great work in his life. Nash had an eye disease that required him to stay in a dark room for many hours each day. While in the darkened, isolated room, he had learned the secret of prayer. Afterward, he devoted himself to an intercessory prayer ministry.

Since Charles had not trained for the regular ministry, he was content to preach in small, out-of-the-way places. Soon, he secured a ministry in the district of Evans Mills, New York, particularly in the town of LeRay. He also preached in Antwerp, a small town of about 660 adults located roughly eighteen miles northeast of Evans Mills. He had a contract with the Female Missionary Society that required him to spend alternate Sundays at Antwerp.

When he first arrived in April 1824, he discovered that no religious services were being held in Antwerp. The area was known as Hell's Acres because of its general wickedness. The town did have a Presbyterian church, but it did not have a regular pastor. A Presbyterian elder's living five miles or so from the town would come to the church on Sunday and preach. The road he traveled, however, took him through a Universalist community, and they were so against the elder's going to preach, they would even take the wheels off his buggy to prevent him from keeping his preaching engagement.

Meanwhile in LeRay, people seemed very interested in what Charles had to say and thronged to hear him. They said they liked his preaching and hoped that the church would grow and that they would be visited by a revival.

Although people regularly came under conviction, still they made no outward profession of Christ, and Charles admitted, "I was very much dissatisfied." He let the people know that he was not there simply to bring them interesting and enjoyable sermons but to see their souls saved.

One day as he began preaching in his blunt style, Charles issued an ultimatum to his flock:

Now I must know your minds, and I want that you who have made up your minds to become Christians and will give your pledge to make your peace with God immediately should rise up; but that, on the contrary, those of you who are resolved that you will not become Christians, and wish me so to understand, and wish Christ so to understand, should sit still. You who are now willing to pledge to me and to Christ that you will immediately make your peace with God, please rise up. On the contrary, you that mean that I should understand that you are committed to remain in your present attitude, not to accept Christ—those of you that are of this mind, may sit still.

The people sat still in shocked disbelief. No preacher had ever admonished them in this fashion. Charles continued: "Then you are committed. You have taken your stand. You have rejected Christ and His gospel; and ye are witnesses one against the other, and God is witness against you all. This is explicit, and you may remember as long as you live, that you have thus publicly committed yourselves against the Savior, and said, 'We will not have this man, Christ Jesus, to reign over us.' "

Then the congregation rose up together in anger and started to leave. Charles stopped preaching, and when he did so, they paused and looked back at him. Charles said, "I am sorry for you; and will preach to you once more, the Lord willing, tomorrow night."

Charles was stunned by his own words and actions. A cloud of depression had settled over him when a Baptist deacon, who had remained behind, came up to him. He took the startled minister by the hand, announcing, "Brother Finney, you have got them. They cannot rest under this, rely upon it. I believe you have done the very thing that needed to be done, and that we shall see the results."

The following day found the deacon and Charles praying and fasting; they prayed separately in the morning and together in the afternoon. Increasingly, Charles realized the importance of prayer in his ministry. Through intercession, he knew that all of God's blessings were available; but without prayer, the results would be few.

Meanwhile, the townspeople were filled with anger and a desire to retaliate. They were considering stern measures against Pastor Finney. Possibilities discussed included tarring and feathering him; riding him out of town on a rail; and giving him his walking papers. Charles discovered later that "some of them cursed me; and said that I had put them under oath, and made them swear that they would not serve God; that I had drawn them into a solemn and public pledge to reject Christ and His gospel."

Nevertheless, the afternoon of what Charles had said would be his last sermon to these people, he met with the Baptist deacon in a grove, and they spent the entire afternoon praying. In Charles's own words, "Just at evening, the Lord gave us great enlargement, and promise of victory. Both of us felt assured that we had prevailed with God; and that, that night, the power of God would be revealed among the people."

As the two men walked back through the village, many people were making their way toward the church. At meeting time, the small building was packed to overflowing. All the town's activities had stopped.

Charles had given no thought to what he would say that evening, and, in fact, this was his customary procedure. As he looked out over the people and realized that the place was packed to capacity, he sensed that "the Holy Spirit was upon me, and I felt confident that when the time came for action I should know what to preach." Then he stood up and, without any preliminary singing or praying, said to the crowd, " 'Say ye to the righteous that it shall be well with him; for they shall eat the fruit of their doings. Woe to the wicked! it shall be ill with him; for the reward of his hands shall be given him.' "

The next events amazed even Charles: "The Spirit of God came upon me with such power that it was like opening a battery upon them. For more than an hour, and perhaps for an hour and a half, the word of God came through me to them in a manner that I could see was carrying all before it. It was a fire and a hammer breaking the rock; and as the sword that was piercing to the dividing asunder of soul and spirit. I saw that a general conviction was spreading over the whole congregation. Many of them could not hold up their heads." Charles sensed that the entire congregation was "committed against the Lord," and so he did not call that night for any commitments to God. Instead he told them a meeting would be held the following night and dismissed them.

As people began to leave, Charles noticed one woman who appeared to be fainting and was being helped by some friends. Having discernment, the evangelist realized the woman was not physically ill but so gripped by conviction, she could not speak. The situation stunned Charles, for he knew the woman to be a faithful church member and the sister of a missionary.

Instead of going to his own place that evening, Charles spent the night with another family. The next morning he discovered that many people had been looking for him throughout the night. Such turmoil of soul had seized the people, they could not sleep. Even the woman under conviction confessed that for sixteen hours, she could not sleep. She admitted that she had been deceived all the years of her faithful church attendance. Under Charles's convicting preaching, she had come face-to-face with God's absolute holiness and her sinfulness. All over town, people were undergoing similar experiences. Revival had come.

Soon, opposition reared its head. Several Deists seemed determined to thwart the moving of God. But Charles planned his strategy. He met with them and preached a direct and convincing sermon opposing their views. To his joy, nearly every Deist at the meeting made a profession of faith.

Opposition came from other quarters, as well. At one of the meetings, a man appeared with a loaded gun, intent on killing the evangelist. Another time, Charles dealt with "an old man, who was not only an infidel, but a great railer at religion. He was very angry at the revival movement. I heard every day of his railing and blaspheming, but took no public notice of it. He refused altogether to attend meeting. But in the midst of the opposition, and when his excitement was great, while sitting one morning at the table, he suddenly fell out of his chair in a fit of apoplexy. A physician was immediately called, who, after a brief examination, told him that he could live but a very short time; and that if he had anything to say, he must say it at once. He had just strength and time, as I was informed, to stammer out, 'Don't let Finney pray over my corpse.' This was the last of the opposition in that place."

A short distance from the village of Evans Mills was a German community. Although the people had a church and many members, they had no regular minister, so they began attending Charles's meetings. They were accustomed to having a minister visit them once each year to administer the ordinances of baptism and communion. He would also listen to the children say their catechism and answer doctrinal questions. If they did so correctly, they would be admitted to church membership. The adult members assumed that these procedures would make the children Christians.

Soon they were captured by the revival spirit and wanted Charles to come preach at their church, which he gladly did. He was amazed to discover that nearly the entire German community turned out to hear him preach. When he preached to them, Charles chose the text: "Without holiness no man shall see the Lord." He showed them, first of all, what holiness was not—including everything they considered to be religion. Then, he showed them what holiness is, and what was meant by seeing the Lord. Last of all, he showed them why those who had no holiness could never see the Lord. The effect was amazing; within days, the whole community came under conviction of sin and the need for Christ.

Charles remarked about the situation: "In a very few days it was found that the whole settlement was under conviction; elders of the church and all were in the greatest consternation, feeling that they had no holiness. At their request I appointed a meeting for inquiry, to give instruction to inquirers. This was in their harvest time. I held the meeting at one o'clock in the afternoon, and found the house literally packed. People had thrown down the implements with which they were gathering their harvest, and had come into the meeting. As many were assembled as could be packed in the house." Later, a gratified Charles noted that "the revival among the Germans resulted in the conversion of the whole church, I believe, and of nearly the whole community of Germans. It was one of the most interesting revivals I have ever witnessed."

During the time of revival in this area, the man known as Father Nash reappeared. Charles had met him earlier when he had come before the presbytery. Father Nash had what he called a praying list, which contained the names of people he wished to pray for. Charles said of him, "His gift of prayer was wonderful, and his faith almost miraculous." Before long, Charles and Father Nash would combine their ministries of preaching and prayer to reap wonderful results.

As the revival continued in the Evans Mills district, Charles became more and more concerned about the methods he used to promote the revival and bring about conversions. He allowed only the accepted meetings of the day to take place: regular preaching services, prayer meetings, conferences, and other gatherings of inquirers regarding their salvation. Of course, he urged much private prayer as well. Even though Charles was young and without much experience, he wanted to be cautious and handle things in a dignified way.

Because of Charles's caution, emotional excess which marked other revivals of the time did not occur in his meetings. Further, he placed his emphasis on the love of God and what Christ had done for us. He familiarized himself with Jonathan Edwards's revival literature from the previous century and followed his example in many of his sermons. Charles's meetings were generally quite orderly. At prayer meetings, Charles insisted that only one person pray at a time and that short breaks take place after long periods of prayer. This would head off any undue emotion being generated.

Charles was not an emotional preacher, even though emotions could be aroused in the midst of a revival—especially among those who were under conviction of sin. He preached primarily to the intellect since he felt that preaching to the emotions was dangerous. Emotions could overcome the intellect and the will, which were under a person's control. He argued that enthusiasm and excitement are genuine only when they encounter the truth. Here, Charles differentiated between what he termed "animal feeling" and "spiritual feeling."

Charles continued preaching in Antwerp during this time. He arranged to use the school building for services. Antwerp had a church house, but the village hotelkeeper had the keys to the building and was so opposed to Charles's ministry that he refused to open it up for the evangelist.

On his first Sunday in Antwerp, Charles preached on John 3:16. He must have made a considerable impression because the hotelkeeper gave up the keys so Charles could hold meetings in the regular church house. Before long, people were flocking to the services. Charles made a practice of praying for Antwerp most of the day before he preached there. Finally one Saturday the Lord responded: "'Be not afraid, but speak, and hold not thy peace; for I am with thee, and no man shall set on thee to hurt thee. For I have much people in this city.'"

Relieved, Charles knew the meetings would go well. Not long after, revival visited Antwerp as it had in other areas of the Evans Mills district, and a great change took place in the people.

An interesting event took place in another school building service about three miles from Antwerp. The godly old man who had invited Charles to speak stood in much contrast to the unbelieving community in which he lived. Charles knew little about the area or the man who had asked him to speak, but he agreed to come. So the service was arranged for five o'clock on a Monday evening.

Charles decided to walk to the school, since it was just three miles. He had not realized how tired he was from the day before and had to rest some before arriving at the school—he knew he should have taken his horse! But he forced himself to continue and arrived at just the right time for the service. The place was filled to capacity, and Charles had to stand and preach from the doorway.

The service began with the people singing a hymn, but they were dreadful singers! Charles, with his sensitive hearing and musical background, had to put his hands over his ears to block out the awful sounds. He was beside himself, and by the time they finished singing, Charles got on his knees and prayed a desperate prayer. He soon sensed the Holy Spirit's presence in the room.

Charles had not given any thought to his sermon subject, which was not that unusual for him. When he got up from his knees, however, the text came to him: "Up, get you out of this place; for the Lord will destroy this city." He told the people the verse was about God's judgment on Sodom and Gomorrah because of their sin and wickedness. Suddenly he became aware of the people's rising anger. They seemed so disturbed, he thought they might attack him.

After he had preached but a short time, Charles noticed "an awful solemnity" covering the people. Amazed, he later recalled: "The congregation began to fall from their seats in every direction, and cried for mercy. If I had had a sword in each hand, I could not have cut them off their seats as fast as they fell. Indeed nearly the whole congregation were either on their knees or prostrate, I should think, in less than two minutes from this first shock that fell upon them. Every one prayed for himself, who was able to speak at all."

He was unable to continue. The people were crying out for mercy and in such agony, they no longer heard anything he said. Then he noticed the old man who invited him, and called out to him, "Can't you pray?" With that, the man fell on the floor and poured out his heart to God.

When the man's prayer was over, Charles spoke as loudly as he could to the people: "You are not in hell yet; and now let me direct you to Christ." For a few minutes he tried to tell them about the gospel, but few paid any attention, they were in such pain. Charles's own heart simply overflowed with joy at the way God was working among people who had moments before been so hostile.

As soon as he could control his own feelings, Charles began to move from one person to another, whispering in their ears the message of God's love in Jesus Christ. As he dealt with them, a wonderful peace settled in their hearts, and they began to pray for others.

Eventually, he had to leave to preach another service in Antwerp. He asked the old man to be in charge. There was so much interest and there were so many needy souls that Charles felt it would be wrong to dismiss the meeting just because he couldn't be there. It continued the rest of the night. The next day the people moved to a private home, so the schoolchildren could use their building for classes.

The following afternoon, the people sent for the evangelist to come back and meet with them. When he arrived the second time, Charles learned why the people had become so angry the day before when he quoted the verse about God's judgment on Sodom. Their community was named Sodom, and there was only one pious man in the town. They called that man Lot, and he was the old man who had invited Charles to preach.

The revival spirit that swept through the schoolhouse proved to be typical of the meetings in Antwerp and other neighboring villages as well. By now, Charles showed himself adept at defending the faith and stilling his opposition—especially the Universalists. As conversions increased and the revival spread, a young man by the name of Denning was called to minister. Charles now felt that he could leave Antwerp. He wished to preach more at Evans Mills.

The Female Missionary Society wanted Charles to continue with them, even though his time was nearly up. After much prayer, he agreed to stay. A whole new chapter in his exciting life, however, was about to begin.

seven

I n October 1824, Charles went to Whitestown, New
York, to marry Lydia Root Andrews. The two first met
at the home of Mrs. Sarah Kirkland of Utica, New
York. Charles had come to receive his commission from
the Female Missionary Society; Lydia had arrived to visit
an aunt who was attending the commissioning meeting.
Born in 1804, Lydia was thirteen years younger than
Charles. At the age of eleven, she had found Christ under
the ministry of the Reverend John Frost. Lydia's delight in
spiritual things made her a desirable match for Charles.

She had prayed for his conversion for many years
during the time he had been a skeptical unbeliever. He
did not realize her concern for him at the time, and it is
not known how she knew of him and had begun to pray
for him. It is possible their two families knew each other
from an earlier time since the towns of Whitestown and
Kirkland are located rather near each other.

After meeting Lydia in Utica, Charles struggled to put her out of his mind. Even when he prayed, his thoughts tended to stray to the beautiful young woman. When this first happened, he thought it sinful to be thinking about her instead of the Lord. But soon he began to understand that the Lord had brought Lydia into his life intending her to be his wife.

A short time later, Charles asked Lydia to marry him. Looking at her earnestly, he said, "Lydia, you're only twenty, I'm thirty-two. Would you be content to be the wife of a minister?"

Happily, she replied, "Oh, Charles. I've loved you secretly ever since I was a small girl. I was one of the band that prayed for your conversion. And I am afraid I prayed as much that you might be mine as that you might be saved." Shortly after that, the two were married.

After the wedding, the couple left for a brief honeymoon. Then Charles left his bride in Whitestown, while he rode back to Evans Mills to arrange for their move to that town. They planned on Charles returning the following week to get Lydia.

While in Evans Mills, however, Charles received word from Christians in nearby Perch River, requesting that he come and preach to them. He had spent some time in Perch River shortly before his marriage, and in their message to him, they said there had been revival stirrings in their area ever since those meetings. Charles usually was unable to resist such appeals, so he agreed to go the following Tuesday evening. Then the next day he would travel on to Whitestown to get his new bride as they had planned.

When Charles preached at Perch River on Tuesday night, however, the Spirit of God moved greatly upon the people. Charles could not leave. It didn't take long for him to realize that he would be unable to return to Whitestown for Lydia. The revival spread to Brownville, a village several miles from Perch River. There were nearly two thousand adults in the town, and the believers urged Charles to come and minister to them. He felt impressed to go.

He realized he needed to decide what to do about Lydia. He knew he would be involved in the revival for several weeks, and it would not be long until cold weather set in, making travel difficult. Would Lydia understand? If he stayed, it could mean months of separation, and they had had only a brief honeymoon together. No doubt it was difficult for Charles to write to her and tell her about this new development.

But from the outset of their marriage, Lydia showed an understanding and gracious spirit. Although it was probably not easy for her, she wanted what was best for Charles. She said she would wait for him to get her when "God seemed to open the door."

The work in Brownville proved difficult. The people, including even the pastor of the church that had invited Charles, seemed cold and indifferent. Sometimes the minister and his wife would be absent from the services, and Charles would learn they had attended a party. It was difficult for Charles to work in such a cold place with his new wife so far away. He admitted later, "I labored there that winter with great pain and had many serious obstacles to overcome." Even though the revival did not seem to affect people as deeply as the ones at Antwerp and Evans Mills, there were some significant conversions.

In the spring of 1825, Charles left Brownville in his horse and buggy to go to Lydia. They had been married for six months, and the letters they were able to send through the minimal mail service were a poor substitute for being together. Charles felt a surge of joy. At last he was on his way to see his wife. He had gone about fifteen miles when he realized that his horse was smooth-shod, and it was dangerous to travel like that on the slippery roads. So he stopped at the small village of LaRayville to have his horse reshod.

While he waited for the blacksmith to shoe his horse, Charles was approached by the townspeople and asked to preach at one o'clock that afternoon. As usual, he gave in to their requests. He never could resist an invitation to preach. Since there was no church in town, the meeting took place in the schoolhouse. When he arrived early that afternoon, the building was filled with people eager to hear him.

After Charles had preached a short time, the Holy Spirit fell on the townspeople. They begged Charles to stay, and he wanted to. But what should he do about his patient wife? They had been married for six months and had scarcely seen each other. The townspeople won out, and Charles said he would preach another night. The revival began to spread, and more meetings were arranged. Charles decided that he would send a good friend to go for Lydia. At long last, the young couple were reunited. The revival continued to spread, and within a few weeks, it seemed that most of the population of LaRayville had been converted.

Incredibly when Lydia rejoined her husband, she did not appear upset over the strange introduction the past six months had given her to married life. She seemed to be understanding, taking everything in stride. Friends described their marriage as that of a "lovable couple." Charles, according to these friends, provided the seriousness for their relationship, while Lydia brought the sunshine.

Lydia struggled at times to adjust to life with such a famous and powerful preacher. Sometimes, however, her husband frightened Lydia. She made a point of telling him on one occasion: "Oh my dear, though I know you love me, yet you are terrifying when the power of God comes upon you. You stand there like a mighty angel, shouting the Gospel and wielding the flashing sword of judgment."

The young couple would face adjustments throughout their marriage. Lydia's willingness to counterbalance Charles's occasional pessimism was one of her strongest characteristics.

As Charles finished his last days in LaRayville, his good friend Father Nash came to see him. By this time, the two were fast friends, and Father Nash prayed much for the evangelist's meetings.

Although Father Nash was the subject of some criticism such as "he prays too loud," he shrugged it off. But at times the old man prayed out loud, and sometimes he bordered on being downright noisy. Even when he closed himself in his room or prayed in the woods, people could easily hear him.

One time when he was working with Charles, Father Nash went into the woods to pray. As usual, he prayed loudly, crying out to God. It so happened that someone who opposed the revival overheard him, and even though he could not understand one word in the old man's prayer, he knew who it was and what he was doing. At once, the man came under conviction and found no relief until he gave his life to Christ.

After the meetings at LaRayville, Charles received an invitation to preach in the town of Rutland. Father Nash traveled with the Finneys to this next meeting place. Again God poured out His Spirit. An interesting new development in Charles's ministry occurred during these meetings—one that still impacts modern evangelism. Charles explained what happened: "At the close of the sermon, I did what I do not know I had ever done before, called upon any who would give their hearts to God, to come forward and take the front seat."

Charles's issuing this call branded him as a forerunner of modern evangelism. Today, we recognize what he did as an invitation to accept the gospel, but such an action was unheard of prior to that time. The invitation, and other evangelistic means that Charles adopted, came to be known in time as Finney's "new measures."

While in Rutland, Charles kept thinking of a revelation he had received from God during those long winter months in Brownville: "God revealed to me, all at once, in a most unexpected manner, the fact that He was going to pour out His Spirit at Gouverneur, and that I must go there and preach. Of the place I knew absolutely nothing, except that, in that town, there was so much opposition manifested to the revival in Antwerp, the year before."

Although he still had two or three appointments to preach in the area of Rutland, Charles wanted to know something of Gouverneur. He thought it would be good for them to travel there next. So he said to Father Nash, "You must go to Gouverneur and see what is there, and come back and make your report." After being gone about three days, Nash returned, and said that he "had found a good many professors of religion, under considerable exercise of mind, and that he was confident that there was a good deal of the Spirit of the Lord among the people." He added, however, that "they were not aware what the state of things really was."

So Charles sent Father Nash on ahead to Gouverneur to tell the people when to expect him. The preacher had to ride about thirty miles in a driving rain storm to reach the town, and when he arrived, a judge told him he thought the night's meeting had been called off because of the weather. But Charles went on to the meeting place and found it packed with people.

Charles had not spent time preparing for the meeting, but as he remarked, "The Lord gave me a text, and I went into the pulpit and let my heart out to the people. The word took powerful effect. That was manifest to everybody, I think. I dismissed the meeting, and that night got some rest."

Opposition to the meeting, however, had already begun. The first person to challenge the preacher was a well-known doctor in town who managed the local hotel. The next day as Charles mingled with the townspeople, he met the doctor at the tailoring shop. The doctor, who was a Universalist, let Charles know that he disagreed with him on certain points.

But the evangelist was wiser than when he'd first begun preaching, so he said he would be willing to have a discussion if they could agree on the method. Charles told him: "First, we should take up one point at a time, and discuss it till we had settled it, or had no more to say upon it, and then another, and another, confining ourselves to the point immediately in debate; secondly, that we should not interrupt each other, but each one should be at liberty to give his views upon the point, without interruption; and thirdly, that there should be no cavilling or mere banter, but that we should observe candor and courtesy, and give to every argument due weight, on whichsoever side it was presented. I knew they were all of one way of thinking." Charles understood that the group in the tailor's shop had come together to uphold each other's views and to best him.

By this time, Charles Finney had learned how to set up a debate properly. He no longer relished debate unless exact terms and methods were agreed upon. He knew, too, how aggressive Universalists could be, but he sensed that he owed the doctor an accurate response to his questions about the gospel. Charles's skillful training and experience as a lawyer and his own argumentative expertise soon helped him to best the doctor, who went home looking downcast.

At home, the doctor was restless and paced up and down. His wife, a dedicated Christian, asked him, "What is the matter?"

The doctor looked at her and retorted, "Nothing."

"Doctor, have you seen Mr. Finney this morning?" she asked.

Her question troubled him and caused him abruptly to burst into tears. "Yes," he replied, "and he has turned my weapons on my own head."

With that, the doctor's agony and conviction became intense. Charles observed about him that "as soon as the way was opened for him to speak out, he surrendered himself up to his convictions, and soon after expressed hope in Christ. In a few days his companions were brought in, one after the other, till, I believe, the revival made a clean sweep of them."

After he dealt with the doctor and the Universalists, Charles had another situation to handle. There were two churches in the community, a Baptist and a Presbyterian, but only the Baptist church had a pastor. When revival broke out under Charles's preaching, the Baptists began to oppose it—perhaps because the evangelist did not emphasize baptism by immersion. Of course, Charles was perfectly willing to immerse individuals and had done so on a number of occasions. Since he always desired to keep unity in his meetings, the evangelist and his praying partners began to bring the situation before the Lord.

One Sunday, several young Baptist men marched into the revival meeting intending to stir up trouble. The air was filled with tension as the service started, yet the men remained quiet. All at once Father Nash stood up, struck the pew in front of him with his fist, and with flashing eyes glared at the young men. He proclaimed loudly: "Now, mark you, young men! God will break your ranks in less than one week, either by converting some of you, or by sending some of you to hell. He will do this

85

as certainly as the Lord is my God!"

The meeting place became "still as death," according to Charles. He regretted that Father Nash had gone so far, but the thing was done. Father Nash had committed himself.

However, as Charles noted, "On Tuesday morning of the same week, the leader of these young men came to me, in the greatest distress of mind. He was all prepared to submit; and as soon as I came to press him he broke down like a child, confessed, and manifestly gave himself to Christ. Then he said, 'What shall I do, Mr. Finney?' I replied, 'Go immediately to all your young companions, and pray with them, and exhort them, at once to turn to the Lord.' He did so; and before the week was out, nearly if not all of that class of young men, were hoping in Christ."

Many other conversions took place at Gouverneur, so many that as Charles noted, "The great majority of them [the Gouverneur community] were converted to Christ."

From Gouverneur, Charles traveled on to De Kalb, a village about sixteen miles to the north with an adult population of 355. An old feud had continued to fester between the Presbyterians and the Methodists. Some years before, the Methodists had had a revival, with people literally fainting under the conviction of sin. But the Presbyterians, far more rigorous in their religious expression, were dismayed at such emotional manifestations. The Methodists, however, considered their expressions genuine. When Charles arrived in the community, everyone thought the old animosities had been forgotten, but they were not. They were lying just below the surface waiting to erupt.

As the revival opened in De Kalb under Charles Finney's preaching, a man fell from his seat "under the power of God." People gathered around to help. Charles thought he was a Methodist and was concerned that the old feud would flare up and dampen the Holy Spirit's impact. Much to Charles's amazement, however, the man who had fallen was a leader in the Presbyterian Church. Several other instances of people "falling under the power of God" occurred during the services. Each time, the person was a Presbyterian. These episodes led to a wonderful healing between the members of the Presbyterian and the Methodist churches. It also drew the two churches together in new unity.

As the revival movement continued, tremendous manifestations of God's power occurred. At times it was so great that Charles could not even see to preach. He would explain that all he did was "sit still and see the salvation of God." With the numerous conversions and the order maintained throughout the meetings, the evangelist had to admit he had never witnessed such an outpouring of God's power.

Outstanding characteristics of many of the converts were their honesty and humility. Two men who came into an afternoon meeting provided a wonderful example of lives changed through this revival. Charles knew the one man, an elder, but the other was a stranger to him. As soon as the man entered the room, he looked at Charles, came straight toward him, and lifted him up in his arms, saying, "God bless you! God bless you!" He then turned to the congregation and told them what the Lord had just done for his soul.

Charles noted that "his countenance was all in a glow; and was so changed in his appearance, that those that knew him were perfectly astonished at the change. His son who had not known of this change in his father, when he saw and heard him, rose up and was hastening out of the church. His father cried out, 'Do not leave the house, my son; for I never loved you before.' He went on to speak; and the power with which he spoke was perfectly astonishing. The people melted down on every side; and his son broke down almost immediately."

Father Nash rejoined Charles during the De Kalb awakening. The two worked very well together, and the evangelist relied heavily on his friend's prayers. As Nash prayed in his loud, boisterous manner, he received considerable criticism from some of the community. One critic claimed Nash used the term "God Almighty" sixty-three times in one public prayer. But others wondered why the critic was spending prayer time counting such things.

The whole community became caught up in intercession for the revival. The attitude of prayer that prevailed in De Kalb was unusual and marked the entire revival. Groups of Christians even gathered in small groups on the streets and would fall on their knees in fervent prayer.

Before they ministered in the De Kalb awakening, Charles and Lydia were used to walking from their host's home to the church services. For all the good that Charles did in his preaching, he and Lydia actually had few material possessions. But while in De Kalb, a wealthy Presbyterian elder presented them with a new horse and buggy. By the time of the October 1825 Presbyterian Synod meeting in Utica, they were able to ride in style.

The year of 1825 was important for the Mohawk Valley of western New York. One of the most significant events took place when the governor symbolically emptied a keg of Lake Erie water into New York Harbor, officially opening the Erie Canal. But a much more significant event happened as revival began to sweep over much of western New York.

While many evangelists preached during this revival, none was more used of God than Charles Finney. He had matured considerably from the raw, country preacher who first appeared at his ordination. He had learned how to handle opposition. Perhaps more important, his theological concepts were now well-formed and became useful in his "new measures."

Charles had learned that he was completely dependent on prayer for the moving of God's Spirit. Now, all was in readiness for the next move of God in the revival explosion that would come to the state of New York. The instrument God had prepared to usher it in was also ready in the person of Charles Finney.

eight

After leaving the 1825 Utica Synod meeting, the
Finneys traveled to the small town of Western,
New York, in Oneida County. When Charles began
to preach, revival broke out, and an awakening began to
spread throughout the entire area. The several towns that
benefitted from his ministry were not the leading cities of
America, but it was through this movement of the Holy
Spirit that the relatively unknown lawyer-preacher came
to more prominent attention of the general public.

When Lydia and Charles first arrived in Western, they
greatly enjoyed the beauty of the place. Located on the
eastern edge of Oneida Lake, Western was perfectly situated. The moral and spiritual atmosphere of Western,
however, fell short of its lovely surroundings. Sabbath-
breaking, a serious offence in early nineteenth-century
America, proved to be quite common.

The Finneys had originally gone to Western to visit Charles's former pastor and teacher at Adams, the Reverend George Gale. Because of health, Pastor Gale had moved to a farm near Western. As they rode along toward Western, they met Mr. Gale in his carriage on his way to Utica. Charles was amazed at his old pastor's greeting. "He leaped from his carriage and said, 'God bless you, Brother Finney! I was going down to the synod to see you. You must go home with me; I cannot be denied. I do not believe that I ever was converted; and I wrote the other day to Adams, to know where a letter would reach you, as I wanted to open my mind to you on the subject.' " Charles was impressed by his old pastor's earnestness and consented to preach in Western.

Unknown to Charles, the Christians in Western had been praying for a long time that God would revive them. But Charles was appalled when he first heard them pray at a meeting of about twelve church leaders. Their prayers were cold and lifeless. They reminded him of his preconversion days in Adams.

To his dismay, "The meeting was opened by one of the elders, who read a chapter in the Bible, then a hymn, which they sung. After this he made a long prayer, or perhaps I should say an exhortation, or gave a narrative —I hardly know what to call it. He told the Lord how many years they had been holding that prayer-meeting weekly, and that no answer had been given to their prayers. He made such statements and confessions as greatly shocked me. After he had done, another elder took up the same theme. He read a hymn, and after singing, engaged in a long prayer, in which he went over

91

very nearly the same ground, making such statements as the first one had omitted." Another elder followed the first two with a similar procedure.

Poor Charles! The elders were ready to dismiss the meeting, when they turned to the evangelist to ask if he had a word. When Charles stood up, he had no idea what he would say, except that he started preaching with their own prayers, statements, and confessions as his text. He dissected their words and berated them, asking if they did not understand that their prayer meeting was a mock prayer meeting. Had they come together to mock God by implying that all the blame of what had been passing all this time was because of His sovereignty?

At first the people looked angry. Some said later they were on the point of getting up and going out. But as Charles pressed home to them their own prayers and confessions, one of the elders—the leader among them—burst into tears, exclaiming, "Brother Finney, it is all true!" With that, the man fell upon his knees and wept aloud.

This act seemed to signal the others to follow suit, and every man and woman went down upon their knees. They wept and confessed and broke their hearts before God. This repentance continued for at least an hour or so.

After this dramatic episode, the people pleaded with the evangelist to stay and preach on the Sabbath. Charles believed God was speaking to him through the people and agreed to do so. The prayer meeting had been held on Thursday night, and on Friday, Charles felt his mind "greatly exercised." He went frequently to the church to engage in secret prayer and had a "mighty hold on God."

The news that Charles Finney would be preaching on

the Sabbath spread through the community, and when he preached on Sunday, the church was full of eager listeners. As he preached, "God came down with great power upon the people" and "it was manifest to everybody that the work of grace had begun. I made appointments to preach in different parts of the town, in schoolhouses, and at the center, during the week; and the work increased from day to day."

To Charles's delight, people were moved to pray throughout the area. The women of the church in particular devoted themselves to interceding for others. One man confided his concern about his wife to the evangelist: "Brother Finney, I think my wife will die. She is so exercised in her mind that she cannot rest day or night, but is given up entirely to prayer. She has been all morning in her room, groaning and struggling in prayer; and I am afraid it will entirely overcome her strength."

Trying to be of help, Charles went home with the man. They entered the house and walked into the sitting room. When she heard the preacher's voice, the woman came out of the bedroom, and as Charles observed it: "Upon her face was a most heavenly glow. Her countenance was lighted up with a hope and a joy that were plainly from heaven."

The woman looked at the evangelist with eyes aglow and said, "Brother Finney, the Lord has come! This work will spread all over this region! A cloud of mercy overhangs us all; and we shall see such a work of grace as we have never yet seen."

The woman's husband seemed puzzled, but Charles,

too, had the assurance that God would do a great work in the community. The work spread. Charles was moved to new depths in prayer and personal ministry. He spent hours visiting those who were anxious about their relationship with Christ. Coming back exhausted to the Reverend Gale's house after a full day, Charles experienced a great burden to pray for those he had ministered to. Since he prayed aloud and did not wish to disturb his hosts, Charles had spread a buffalo robe in the hayloft where he could let God alone hear his voice.

On a cold day in November, Charles arrived home bone weary, yet with a great need to pray. He sought the Lord for some time in his hayloft prayer closet until he had the assurance that God had heard him and victory would be forthcoming. Upon receiving the peace of assurance, he lapsed into a deep sleep. After some time, Pastor Gale, quite concerned, came out to check on his guest. He found Charles in such a deep sleep that he called out: "Brother Finney, are you dead?"

When he was thoroughly awake, Charles admitted he had not realized he had fallen asleep, nor how long he slept. He did acknowledge, however, that "my mind was calm and my faith unwavering. The work would go on, of that I felt assured."

While the evangelist stayed with the Reverend Gale in Western, the pastor again told him that he did not believe he had ever been converted. He shared his reasoning with Charles and told him that "he had firmly believed, as he had so frequently urged upon me, that God would not bless my labors, because I would not preach what he regarded as the truths of the gospel. But when he found that the Spirit of God did accompany my labors, it led him to the conclusion that he was wrong; and this led him to such an overhauling of his whole state of mind, and of his views as a preacher, as resulted in his coming to the conclusion that he had never been converted, and did not understand the gospel himself."

During the revival at Western, Pastor Gale attended most of the meetings. Charles recorded: "He told me he had come into an entirely different state of mind in regard to his own soul, and had changed his views of the Gospel, and thought I was right. He said he thanked God that he had had no influence with me, to lead me to adopt his views; that I should have been ruined as a minister if he had prevailed. From this time he became a very efficient worker, so far as his health would permit, in the revival in that region of the country."

Many people besides Charles were battling in prayer for Western. As a result, numerous individuals experienced profound conversions. One person who underwent a dramatic change was a well-known personality in the community known as the Widow Floyd. She was eighty years old and totally blind. Her husband had served as a Revolutionary War officer and had been one of the signers of the Declaration of Independence. He had been known as a skeptic and had retained his unbelief until he died. When his widow found Christ at the age of eighty, the whole community was amazed.

Some of the people attending the meetings at Western lived in nearby Rome, New York, and the surrounding district. It was not long before the seeds of revival were planted in these areas as well, and the people urged the evangelist to come preach in Rome. At first Charles felt he had made a mistake in consenting to go to Rome, but he said later: "The work went on, spread and prevailed, until it began to exhibit unmistakable indications of the direction in which the Spirit of God was leading from that place. The distance to Rome was nine miles, I believe. About half-way, was a small village called Elmer's Hill. There was a large schoolhouse where I held a weekly lecture; and it soon became manifest that the work was spreading in the direction of Rome and Utica."

The invitation to come to Rome had come primarily through the Reverend Moses Gillett, pastor of the Congregational church. He had been a witness to the significant happenings taking place in Western, having arrived just as the awakening had achieved full force. Shaken by the outpouring of God's blessings, Gillett wanted to have a part in the revival. He proposed to Charles that they exchange pulpits for a Sunday. Even though Charles did not wish to do so, reluctantly he agreed. They set a certain Sunday aside for the exchange.

On the day before the exchange, Charles went to Rome with a heavy heart. He greatly regretted having made the agreement. He was concerned that Gillett would not understand how to keep the revival going in Western. And he fretted that Gillett would preach one of the old-style sermons that would have a detrimental effect on the revival. At this point, all he could do was to trust God.

Charles preached three times in Rome on Sunday. The people awakened to a consciousness of sin. The evangelist used as his text: "The carnal mind is enmity against God" (Romans 8:7).

Gillett returned to Rome on Monday. Charles waited for him to tell him the exciting news. Immediately, Gillett wanted to call for inquirers, and he insisted that Charles stay and help conduct the inquirers' meeting. Charles went back to Western for the day, but came back that evening for an anxious meeting (as he sometimes called meetings for people inquiring about the faith), scheduled in a deacon's home. By the time the pastor and evangelist arrived, they found the deacon's large sitting room packed to overflowing. Gillett's amazement did not stop there. Many leading members of his congregation were in the room, inquiring about their souls.

Pastor Gillett started to counsel them, but the atmosphere was so charged with emotion, it seemed the place would explode. Charles, not wanting his revivals to be shallow, picked up where the pastor left off. He told him: "It will not do to continue the meeting in this shape. I will make some remarks, such as they need, and then dismiss them." No effort had been made to stimulate the people emotionally. They were simply responding to the convicting power of the Holy Spirit at work in their lives.

Charles remarked later about the situation: "The work was with such power, that even a few words of conversation would make the stoutest men writhe on their seats, as if a sword had been thrust into their hearts. It would probably not be possible for one who had never witnessed such a scene, to realize what the force of the truth sometimes is, under the power of the Holy Ghost. It was indeed, a sword, and a two-edged sword. The pain that it produced when searchingly presented in a few words of conversation, would create a distress that seemed unendurable."

Taking over from Pastor Gillett, Charles addressed the group in as gentle and quiet a manner as he could, yet he was plain and honest. He called their attention at once to their only remedy and assured them it was a present and all-sufficient remedy. "I pointed them to Christ, as the Savior of the world; and kept on in this strain as long as they could well endure it, which indeed, was but a few moments." He added, "Now please go home without speaking a word to each other. Try to keep silent, and do not break out into any boisterous manifestation or feeling; but go without saying a word, to your rooms." They began to leave. Some were sobbing, others sighing.

Charles accompanied one of the men from the meeting. They maintained their silence until they entered the house. Suddenly the man burst into what Charles called "a loud wailing." The noise brought the whole family to the scene. The man's deep conviction soon spread to all of them. Quickly, the house became filled with prayer. Everyone in the family was saved, and similar scenes were enacted all over town.

Early the next morning, people began coming to Pastor Gillett's house, seeking spiritual help. After eating breakfast quickly, Charles and the pastor went out to see how they could help the people. As they went down the street, Charles said later, "The people ran out from many houses, and begged us to go into their houses. As we could only visit but one place at a time, when we went into a house, the neighbors would rush in and fill the largest room. We would stay and give them instruction for a short time, and then go to another house, and the people would follow us."

The situation was, as Charles termed it, "Extraordinary. Convictions were so deep and universal, that we would sometimes go into a house, and find some in a kneeling posture, and some prostrate on the floor. We visited, and conversed, and prayed in this manner, from house to house, till noon. I then said to Mr. Gillett, 'This will never do; we must have a meeting of inquiry. We cannot go from house to house, and we are not meeting the wants of the people at all.' He agreed with me; but the question arose, where shall we have the meeting?"

Soon, Pastor Gillett approached the proprietor of the hotel in the center of town. An arrangement was made to use the dining room at one o'clock in the afternoon. After lunch, the evangelist and pastor made their way to the hotel. People were flocking to the hotel—some came running, so anxious were they about their souls. Before long, the large dining room was crammed to capacity.

By the time the meeting opened, the same burden of concern that had marked the previous night was evident. The feeling was overwhelming. Some men were so stricken by the remarks that were made, they were unable to walk and had to be taken home by their friends. The meeting lasted till nearly night. Charles noted with considerable reserve: "It resulted in a great number of hopeful conversions, and was the means of greatly extending the work on every side."

In the evening, Charles preached again in the regular church services. Pastor Gillett set up another inquiry meeting for the following morning. This time, he made arrangements to meet at the courthouse, which had a much larger room than the hotel. Again, at the appointed hour, people rushed in, filling the place to capacity. The two men gave instruction for the rest of the day.

Charles followed the same routine the next day when he preached again in the evening. This time Pastor Gillett was able to locate a room in the church that would be large enough for the numerous inquirers. The evening evangelistic services became so powerful that Charles felt he must stay in Rome and preach regularly. For twenty straight nights, with two services on Sunday, he preached the gospel. A prayer meeting and an inquiry meeting dominated every day, and as Charles said, "There was a solemnity throughout the whole place, and an awe that made everybody feel that God was there."

In fact, "Rome was in an extraordinary state of things. Convictions were so deep and universal that we would sometimes go into a house, and find some in a kneeling posture, some prostrate on the carpet, some bathing the temples of their friends with camphor, and rubbing them to keep them from fainting, and as they feared from dying." During the twenty days, at least five hundred conversions were reported.

News of the meetings in Rome spread quickly to neighboring areas. Soon, ministers converged on the scene from outlying areas everywhere. Keeping track of conversions became an impossibility. The only recourse for Charles was to call on those who had been converted during the day to come forward at the close of the evening sermon, confess their new faith publicly, and receive helpful instructions. The continuing development of this "new measure" gave credence to the method used so widely in today's mass evangelism meetings.

To illustrate the tremendous power of the meetings, Charles described a typical event during the Rome awakening:

At one of the morning prayer meetings, the lower part of the church was full. I arose and was making some remarks to the people, when an unconverted man, a merchant, came into the meeting. He came along until he found a seat in front of me, and near where I stood speaking. He had sat but a few moments, when he fell from his seat as if he had been shot. He writhed and groaned in a terrible manner. I stepped to the pew door and saw that it was altogether an agony of mind.

A skeptical physician sat near him. He stepped out of the slip, and came and examined this man who was thus distressed. He felt his pulse, and examined the case for a few moments. He said nothing, but turned away and leaned his head against a post that supported the gallery, and manifested great agitation.

He said afterward that he saw at once that it was distress of mind, and it took his skepticism entirely away. He was soon after hopefully converted. We engaged in prayer for the man who fell in the pew; and before he left the house, I believe his anguish passed away, and he rejoiced in Christ.

God also performed what the evangelist called "some

terrible things in righteousness." Three men stubbornly opposed the Rome meetings. They met one Sunday and spent the entire day drinking and ridiculing the work. Suddenly, one of them fell stone dead. The other two were speechless, convinced that God had judged them for their adamant opposition to the obvious work of the Holy Spirit.

While the work in Rome progressed in a powerful way, excitement sprang up in the surrounding area. The prayers of a pious Christian woman in Utica had already reached out to the Utica community. She was spending days and nights in intercession for an outpouring of the Spirit in her town. Others began to join her in exceptional prayer. Charles, ever sensitive to such signs, realized that God was ready to move in the city. So he went to Utica and began preaching.

The influence of God's Spirit saturated the community, and the meetings overflowed night after night. Father Nash came to intercede in prayer for the revival. Two Presbyterian congregations in Utica were special recipients of the revival, and their pastors, the Reverend Samuel Aiken and the Reverend Samuel Brace, embraced the work wholeheartedly.

At the outset of his time in Utica, Charles took a room in the leading hotel. Before long, the hotel owner and his entire family were converted, together with a large number of the guests. Charles recorded that:

The stages, as they passed through, stopped at the hotel, and so powerful was the impression in the community, that I heard of several cases of persons that just stopped for a meal, or to spend a night, being powerfully convicted or converted before they left the town. Indeed, both in this place and in Rome, it was a common remark that nobody could be in the town, or pass through it, without being aware of the presence of God; that a divine influence seemed to pervade the place, and the whole atmosphere to be instinct [filled] with a divine presence.

An interesting incident took place when Charles visited a cotton mill in Utica. The owner was not a Christian, but he was known as a man of high morals and excellent standing in the community. In addition, Charles's brother-in-law was the superintendent of the mill. Since Charles had preached in the mill's vicinity one evening, he was given a tour through the factory the next day.

As the factory owner, Charles, and his brother-in-law walked through the mill looking at the various stages in the production of cotton cloth, they came to a large room where a number of women were working at the weaving machines. The workers kept looking at Charles, knowing who he was and having heard about the revival that was taking place in the area. Two girls, in particular, seemed taken by his presence, but were laughing lightheartedly.

As Charles recalled: "I went slowly toward them. They saw me coming, and were evidently much excited. One of them was trying to mend a broken thread, and I observed that her hands trembled so that she could not mend it. I approached slowly, looking on each side at the machinery as I passed; but observed that this girl grew more and more agitated, and could not proceed with her work. When I came within eight or ten feet of her, I looked solemnly at her. She observed it, and was quite overcome, and sunk down, and burst into tears. The impression caught almost like powder, and in a few moments nearly all in the room were in tears."

Conviction spread through the whole factory. The owner, deeply moved himself, said to the superintendent, "Stop the mill, and let the people attend to religion; for it is more important that our souls be saved than that this factory run." The factory was shut down, and all the employees gathered into one large room. Charles preached, and as he noted, "A more powerful meeting I scarcely ever attended." The revival swept through the entire group of factory employees until within a few days nearly all were brought to faith in Christ.

Perhaps the most remarkable conversion in Utica was that of Theodore D. Weld. The story of his religious experience reveals again the amazing work of God's Spirit. Weld was a student at Hamilton College in Clinton, New York, which was not far from Utica. The revival in Utica attracted the attention of the Hamilton College community, and many of Hamilton's professors and students attended the revival. Campus talk often centered around the revival.

A leader on campus, Weld was an outstanding student and influential with his fellow students. His Christian heritage, too, was impeccable: His father was a prominent New England minister, and he had a godly praying aunt in Utica. Nevertheless, Weld himself had no use for the gospel and proved to be an outspoken antagonist. When he heard about the Finney revival, Weld used his verbal gifts to fight it. Even though Charles was a complete stranger to Weld, he had nothing good to say about him. When his aunt learned of his antagonism toward Charles and the work of God's Spirit, she grew extremely burdened for her nephew's conversion.

At the invitation of his aunt, Theodore Weld came to Utica for a weekend visit. He made it a point to tell his college friends that he would show them how to sit through a revival meeting unmoved. His plans, however, included attending the morning service when Pastor Aiken preached instead of Charles's afternoon service. His aunt made her own plans and persuaded Charles and Pastor Aiken to exchange their preaching times. Then the aunt put Weld in the middle of the pew, so it would be quite difficult for him to bolt from the service.

As the service began, Pastor Aiken accompanied Charles to the pulpit area. He had pointed Weld out to Charles earlier, and Charles knew of his considerable influence and of his opposition to the meetings. When the evangelist stood to preach, he took as his text, "One sinner destroyeth much good" (Ecclesiastes 9:18). Charles said later that he had never preached on that verse nor heard anyone else preach it. The Holy Spirit had brought it to his mind for that particular occasion.

Charles's sermon produced a marked effect on young Weld. The evangelist noted, "I suppose that I drew a pretty vivid picture of Weld, and of what his influence was, and what mischief he might do." Weld tried several times to climb out of the pew, but whenever he started to move, his aunt would throw herself forward and engage in silent prayer, preventing him from escaping.

She implored him, "Theodore, if you leave, you will break my heart." So he sat there and endured the entire sermon. At sermon's end, Weld finally was free from the evangelist's stinging words.

The next day, Charles went to a store on Genesee Street and whom should he encounter but Theodore Weld! The young man lashed out at the evangelist verbally for nearly an hour. The place filled with townspeople overwhelmed with what they were hearing. The evangelist patiently let the young man continue until he had vented all his anger.

Then Charles drew himself up to his full stature and addressed the young upstart: "Mr. Weld, are you the son of a minister of Christ, and is this the way for you to behave?" That was all he said, but the words pierced like a sword into young Weld's heart. Deeply offended, Weld muttered some final cutting words and marched out of the store.

Charles left the store and walked to Pastor Aiken's home. He had been there only a few minutes when he heard a knock at the door. To his astonishment, there stood Weld. His face was ashen as he began to pour out a most humble confession and apology. Graciously Charles accepted his apology and encouraged him to give his life to Christ. With that, the young student left and went to his aunt's home, much subdued.

She asked him to lead the family in prayer, but as he knelt down, the bitterness rose in him again, even more vicious than before. He attacked the revival with blasphemous words, and his aunt began to shudder. Relentlessly he continued until the lamp oil had burned low. The family was shocked, and his aunt was genuinely concerned and frightened at his outright blasphemy. When Weld finally spent himself, his aunt urged him to give his heart to God.

With that, he flew out and went to his room for the night. But he found it impossible to sleep. His agitation deepened as the hours dragged on. He paced the floor all night. Just as dawn came on, as Weld himself explained later, a great "pressure" came upon him that literally prostrated him. Along with the "pressure," a voice seemed to say, "Repent, repent now!"

Later in the morning his aunt came to his room to find out why he had not come down for breakfast. She found him on the floor, calling himself a "thousand fools." His heart was completely broken. He had met Jesus Christ.

At the evening service, Weld got up and asked if he could say a few words. He made an eloquent, humble, and beautiful confession of Christ. Gone were the tirades and blasphemy against the revival. His life had been radically and wondrously transformed. He acknowledged the stumbling block he had been and said that now his only desire was that his whole life might count for the cause of Christ.

From the time of his striking conversion, Weld became a diligent servant of Christ and one of Charles's biggest supporters. Later on, he was influential in various Christian movements and in abolitionist activities. After that, he entered Lane Seminary in Cincinnati, Ohio, and the rest of his life was used by God in many ways.

Two significant events happened to Charles while he was in Utica. The first occurred when he stayed at Pastor Aiken's home and was introduced to the writings of Jonathan Edwards. Edwards's works about the occurrences of the First Great Awakening had a tremendous impact on the evangelist, altering his theology, preaching, and revival concepts. The other event was the rising of opposition against his "new measures." He would learn, however, to deal with this situation quickly.

By 1826, Charles's name was becoming well-known throughout western New York. The pastor of the First Presbyterian Church of Auburn, Dr. Lansing, visited one of the Utica meetings and witnessed the power of the awakening. Overwhelmed by what he experienced, he invited Charles to preach in Auburn. Since he believed his work was done in Utica, the evangelist followed what he felt to be the Holy Spirit's leading. His caution to wait on God's Spirit meant that he never had to leave in the middle of a revival—he could remain one day or one year as he needed to.

But when Charles went to Auburn, another spirit began to plague him. Some of the religious leaders of a theological seminary in Auburn, along with some professors and students, got together to oppose the revival meetings. Then, a plan to confine Charles and his meetings to the western part of New York was set in motion. Several prominent ministers declared that he would never be allowed to come east and disrupt the churches of New England.

As soon as the evangelist arrived in Auburn, he

learned from various sources that a system of espionage was being carried on that was intended to create a network of ministers and churches to hedge him in and to prevent the spread of the revivals connected with his work.

Charles knew that rumors and false reports had been spread about him and the meetings. He realized he would need to deal with this situation but was not sure what to do. When his ministry in Auburn began, however, the Holy Spirit indicated that he would face some troubling times ahead:

> *I shall never forget what a scene I passed through one day in my room at Dr. Lansing's. The Lord showed me as in a vision what was before me. He drew so near to me, while I was engaged in prayer, that my flesh literally trembled on my bones. I shook from head to foot, under a full sense of the presence of God. At first, and for some time, it seemed more like being on the top of Mount Sinai, amidst its full thunderings, than in the presence of the cross of Christ.*
>
> *Never in my life, that I recollect, was I so awed and humbled before God as then. Nevertheless, instead of feeling like fleeing, I seemed drawn nearer and nearer to God— seemed to draw nearer and nearer to that Presence that filled me with such an unutterable awe and trembling. After a season of great humiliation before him, there came a great lifting up. God assured me that He would be with me and uphold me; that no opposition should prevail*

against me; that I had nothing to do, in regard at all to this matter, but to keep about my work, and wait for the salvation of God.

The passage of Scripture the Spirit of God reminded Charles of, and upon which he trusted, was: "Thou art stronger than I, and hast prevailed" (Jeremiah 20:7). He knew God would see him through this difficult time.

Before he had preached very long in Auburn, the church broke down in confession. The entire church body wanted to publicly acknowledge their backsliding and spiritual poverty, so they prepared a written confession and submitted it to the church. At the time of the document's presentation, the whole congregation stood in agreement, weeping as they did so. After that, the work continued unabated, and many souls were swept into the kingdom of God. In 1831, a number of years later, when Charles returned to Auburn, another powerful revival began. The people of Auburn were always glad to see him and welcomed him wholeheartedly.

Early in the autumn of 1826, the evangelist accepted an invitation from Dr. Nathaniel Beman, as Charles noted "to labor with them for the revival of religion." Charles spent the autumn and winter in Troy, New York, and as often happened in these meetings, "a very earnest spirit of prayer" came forth. A prayer meeting took place daily at eleven o'clock, going from house to house. These prayer services deepened until they were used by God to bring many souls into the kingdom.

At one of the meetings, a bank cashier was so pressed by the spirit of prayer that when the meeting was dismissed, he was unable to rise from his knees. He remained upon his knees, and writhed and groaned in agony. According to Charles, "He said, 'Pray for Mr.____,' president of the bank of which he was cashier. This president was a wealthy, unconverted man. When it was seen that his soul was in travail for that man, the praying people knelt down, and wrestled in prayer for his conversion. As soon as the mind of Mr. S. was so relieved that he could go home, we all retired; and soon after the president of the bank, for whom we prayed, expressed hope in Christ. He had not before this attended any of the meetings; and it was not known that he was concerned about his salvation. But prayer prevailed, and God soon took his case in hand."

In the midst of the revival, a young lady traveled to Troy from New Lebanon in Columbia County. She had come to buy a dress for a ball in her hometown. A cousin in Troy, who was a recent convert because of the Finney revival, invited her to one of the services. Although she did not want to go, she finally gave in to her cousin's urging. The Spirit of God worked mightily that night, and the woman was wondrously converted.

The young woman, dismissing her dress and the ball, returned to New Lebanon and started to work for a revival there. Before long, her father, a deacon in the local church, experienced a revival in his life. Then the woman visited her pastor's daughter, who was not a Christian. She persuaded the young lady to put her faith in Christ, so she, too, became a believer. The two of them began to pray together for others in their community. By the time they had prayed a week, they agreed that Charles Finney should come and preach in New Lebanon. When they went to

Troy to talk with him, he said he would come.

Charles began preaching in New Lebanon, and God blessed the work almost at once. Dramatic conversions were multiplied, and what he called "a great and blessed change" came over the entire community. Most of the leading citizens of the small town were converted.

During the time of the New Lebanon revival, the controversy over Charles's "new measures" was coming to a head. What became known as the Great Western Revivals and Finney's methods were a growing topic of conversation. Letters flew thick and fast between Christians in western New York, who were sympathetic to Charles's revivals and methods, and the leading "Eastern brethren," such as evangelist Ashel Nettleton and pastor Lyman Beecher. The controversy had taken on a life of its own.

Charles knew he needed to do something about the issue, so a date was set in late July 1827 to hold a convention to consider the issue of "measures" in revivals. They decided to hold the convention in New Lebanon. Charles felt assurance from the Lord that he would be ready.

nine

By this time, the Western Revivals had nearly reached their height, and Charles Finney was considered a successful evangelist. He had honed and refined his revolutionary "new measures" until they accomplished what the evangelist had in mind. While the revivals continued to gain strength, however, criticism was also growing in strength and threatened to undo whatever the revivals had achieved.

Earlier, when Charles preached in places like Jefferson and St. Lawrence Counties under the auspices of the Female Missionary Society, he did not receive much notice. One reason was that these places were out of the way; another reason was that he was young and inexperienced and made some mistakes. Although the revivals he preached in those days were powerful and the exciting news was reported in local periodicals, little mention was made of Charles himself in connection with the meetings.

Besides, practically everyone in Jefferson and St. Lawrence Counties had either been converted or was deeply moved by the revivals.

Later, however, when the revival fires began to reach Oneida County, they were getting too impressive to ignore. Also, places like Gouverneur, Utica, and Rome were growing rapidly and becoming some of New York's largest cities. Any revivals in these places would attract attention. Now the name Charles Finney was being mentioned in the same breath as the revivals, and revival news spread as far east as Boston.

The unbelieving community sounded the first alarm about the revival. Different tactics were used—from simple ridicule to acts of violence. When Father Nash mentioned the Oneida revivals on May 11, 1826, he said, "The work of God moved forward in power, in some places against dreadful opposition. Mr. Finney and I have been hanged in effigy. Sometimes the opposition made a noise in the house of God; sometimes they gathered around the house and stoned it, and discharged guns."

The religious opposition to the revivals came from three different sources: the Unitarians, the "old school" Calvinists, and critics of the "new measures." The "new measure" critics represented a wide range of theological thought. Thus, people of various theological beliefs united against Charles and his friends, objecting to the methodologies he used. Incredibly, many of the "new measure" critics were diligent advocates of revivals themselves. A number of them even used some of the "new measure" methods to their own advantage.

While critical voices had been raised against the Finney revivals for some time, they reached a high pitch by the time of the Utica revival. An outstanding spokesman for the opposition was the Reverend William R. Weeks. He was pastor of the Congregational church at Paris Hill in Oneida County, and adhered to the thought of Samuel Hopkins, so he was known as a "Hopkinsian." Hopkins himself followed the ideas of Dr. Nathaniel Emmens, one of the leading "old school" Calvinistic theologians. Weeks had tried to impose his theological ideas on the local believers and churches in Oneida County but without success, so he parted company with them and formed his own group called the "Oneida Association." Following the break, Weeks employed various tactics to disgrace Charles's new measures.

Weeks used different methods to achieve his goal. First, he corresponded with men of influence in New England; in particular, he sought out those who approved of revivals in general. He hoped by persuading these individuals of Charles's "errors" to create a division among the "new school" theologians. Moreover, he started sending detrimental pamphlets and articles that enjoyed a wide circulation. The most damaging pamphlet Weeks wrote contrary to the new measures came out under the title "A Pastoral Letter to the Ministers of the Oneida Association to the Churches under Their Care on the Subject of Revivals of Religion." Since the pamphlet appeared first in Oneida County where the revivals were being held, many people read it.

Cleverly, Weeks did not come right out and condemn revivals. He knew the eastern clergy were usually favorable to them. Jonathan Edwards, a leader in the first Great Awakening during the previous century, had come from New England. Weeks maintained, however, that those historic movements did not contain any outlandish practices (which he considered the new measures to be) since the mature clergy would not allow them. As the opposition gathered momentum, both "old" and "new school" ministers began to side with Weeks, causing the opposition toward Charles to gain ground.

In addition, Weeks worked to incite the "new school" men of New England. Weeks fervently desired to discredit Charles in front of them. He did not have to bother that much with the "old school" people since they had already dismissed the evangelist. Some of the accusations that flew fast and furious were ridiculous things like charging the evangelist with wild emotionalism, weird theology, and bizarre practices. One of the most damaging reports declared that parents were beating their children to force them to become Christians. Finally, Weeks stated that Charles wanted to alienate the position and respect of the pastors and churches where he held revivals.

The "Bunker Hill" pamphlet was published by the Unitarians and widely circulated. Why did the Unitarians and other groups oppose Charles's revivals? The answer most likely is that they relished seeing the orthodox clergy sparring with each other. In the "Bunker Hill" pamphlet, for example, in addition to criticizing the new measures, Charles's foes maligned his character and questioned his motives. The title page of the pamphlet is as follows:

BUNKER HILL CONTEST
A.D. 1826

Between the "Holy Alliance," for the Establishment of
Hierarchy and Ecclesiastical Domination
over the Human Mind
ON THE ONE SIDE,

And the Asserters of Free Inquiry, Bible Religion,
Christian Freedom and Civil Liberty
ON THE OTHER

THE REV. CHARLES FINNEY
"Home Missionary" and High Priest of the Alliance in
the Interior of New York
Headquarters: County of Oneida

Some of the pamphlet's distortions spoke of Charles's "anxious" meetings being held in dark rooms with an atmosphere charged with groans and subdued whispers which brought about false conversions.

The truth about these distortions was that in Charles's early days in the revival ministry, he did not even use the anxious meeting. He invited concerned people to come to the front of the church following dismissal of the service so he could counsel them personally and individually. After the revivals increased in size, the evangelist used the anxious meeting. Nevertheless, the meetings were always orderly.

The "Bunker Hill" pamphlet was purportedly written by a plain farmer from Trenton, New Jersey, but the language was such that a plain farmer of the day could not have written it. Ephraim Perkins's name has been associated with the pamphlet, but it is thought that a man named Henry Ware of Trenton printed it. The pamphlet questioned Charles's personal life as well as the credibility of his new measures.

The best objections to the actual issues involved in the new measures were presented in the Reverend Weeks's pastoral letter. He covered in twenty-nine corresponding points the "evils to be guarded against" in the Finney movement. The problem with Weeks's letter is that he lumped together other itinerant evangelists who were guilty of the wild, bizarre extravagance that he accused Charles of. He included as well a few good pastors who used the new measures with discretion and good results. Weeks did not separate the worthwhile methods from the worthless ones.

In an effort to discount the letter, the Oneida Presbytery printed a tract called "A Narrative of the Revival of Religion in the Country of Oneida." Charles's revivals, according to the tract, took place with less "excitement and passions" and more "wisdom and discretion" than any could recall in any previous meetings. The most significant section appeared under the heading "Means Which Appear to Have Been Blessed in Promoting Revivals," where thirteen such means of blessing were given.

Some of the new measures included in this section were that people "anxious" about their conversion were asked to attend a special meeting for counsel on how to be saved. Charles employed the anxious meeting a great deal in his ministry, finding it most effective. The main purpose of this special kind of meeting was to help people unsure of their salvation to find Christ. Charles never wished to bring on shallow conversions, although he was accused of doing just that. His very theology shows the reverse of shallowness: he believed that people made their own decisions for or against Christ.

Further, when Charles rejected extreme Calvinism, he took a position highly respectful of man's free will. Charles believed that God's Spirit brings conviction to sinners, showing them their need of salvation. People must then make their own "free will" decisions. All that a Christian can do is to point the seeker to God's forgiveness in Christ. So the anxious meeting was set up to provide guidance and help for seekers.

The second point considered by the opposition concerned Charles's method of house-to-house visitation. Incredibly, the evangelist's critics thought the practice of calling on people concerned about their salvation and counseling them on how to receive forgiveness and salvation was much too humanistic.

The third point of contention pertained to the "anxious seat." For Charles to tell people anxious about their relationship to Christ to take a special place in the church building was revolting, in particular to the old school. Doing this, they believed, set aside the work of the Holy Spirit. People were not necessarily called to the anxious seat at the close of a meeting. Often it was suggested they sit in the anxious seat at the outset of the service when no particular emotion was present.

As a point of fact, Charles did not invent the anxious

seat. It is thought to have originated at the turn of the nineteenth century in the Methodist camp meetings as a "mourners' bench." Until the Rochester revival of 1831, Charles did not even use it.

A fourth issue dealt with what Weeks considered "familiarity with God in prayer."

Charles did not pray nor preach in the customary "language of Zion." So his critics called him a "vulgar speaker." Above all, the evangelist wanted to be a communicator. Charles believed that as an ambassador for Christ he needed to communicate clearly and effectively. Because of his belief, he spoke the language of the people.

Since he relied on this principle in preaching, he also used it in prayer. His desire was for people to understand spiritual things clearly—not to be confused about them because of stilted language. Charles knew that God understood plain, simple words, and that no irreverence was involved in addressing Him in common, everyday language.

The fifth point of contention had to do with church membership for new converts. The evangelist stood accused of opening the church doors too soon and allowing new converts to become members before they were ready. When Charles's record came to light, however, not one incident could be found where he pressured pastors into receiving a new convert prematurely. He tried always to abide by the pastors' principles regarding church membership. If a pastor disagreed with Charles's views, Charles respected that.

In addition, studies show that converts who were allowed into the life of the church remained faithful and grew into mature Christians. Historian R. H. Fowler admitted in his study *Historical Sketch of Presbyterianism within the Bounds of the Synod of Central New York* that converts of the Oneida County revival usually offered much to the churches they joined.

The sixth measure which caused the most controversy was allowing women to pray in public. Charles elevated women by using them in revival leadership roles. In the nineteenth century, women's rights were much in the forefront of reforms, and the evangelist expressed a wide range of concerns. He sought after social justice as well as being a zealous revivalist, and he wove these two endeavors into his ministry. Charles thought it both Christian and logical to allow any member of the church, male or female, to serve in whatever capacity he or she was best suited.

His practices, however, shocked traditional church members. Then there were the St. Paul "proof texters" who pointed out Charles's errors of interpretation to him. But Charles simply replied: "I know some have supposed that the Scriptures plainly prohibit the speaking or praying of women in promiscuous assemblies, but I do not so understand the teachings of the Bible."

Charles has even been accused of—or credited with—the whole concept of women participating in public worship. Women, however, were already speaking publicly in Utica when the evangelist came there. He admitted at the time that it was a local custom. In fact, Theodore Weld may have started the practice. Weld admitted that, "I was converted to Christ in the city of Utica during a powerful revival of religion under Brother Finney, and the first time

I ever spoke in a religious meeting, I urged females both to pray and speak if they felt deeply enough to do it, and not to be restrained from it by the fact that they were female."

Another measure that Charles used was praying for people by name in public. Traditionalists simply did not do this. Feelings ran high regarding this practice, particularly among the "old school" theologians who asked, "What if the person named in prayer was not one of the 'elect'?" That question encompassed the real problem.

Even the extended meeting itself presented a problem to some people. For an evangelist to arrive in a community, stay, and preach until revival came was not the way to bring in the kingdom of God. The objections to this practice were mixed. Some said if the meeting were drawn out, it reflected continued interest. But another concern was that pastors and evangelists might deliberately extend a meeting, pretending renewed interest by the people involved. If the meeting were deliberately prolonged, of course, the evangelist and pastor could get credit for a successful revival; but it would also leave the people exhausted and suffering from nervous fatigue. This situation would also make the people vulnerable to spiritual degeneration, fanaticism, and extravagance.

Of course, these arguments contained some truth. But as far as Charles and his revivals were concerned, the concerns did not apply. As soon as he knew the revival had run its course, he would leave immediately. Further, he realized that physical exhaustion and spiritual exhaustion often go hand in hand, so he tried hard not to overextend the people.

Charles could be blamed for some of these abuses, since some of the abusing evangelists were imitating his new measures. Another aspect of the abuses was that Charles implied that if the right methods were used, God would be required to send revival. Some important considerations need to be understood as to why the evangelist insisted on the matters he did.

First of all, the institution of the new measures reveals Charles's reaction to a rigid Calvinism, a Calvinism that emphasized the sovereignty of God to the near-elimination of human responsibility. People were even seen as passive agents when they received the grace of God. The evangelist had never been able to believe in such an approach; as a result, he perhaps swung toward the other extreme. Later, as a mature preacher, he did admit that he had put too much emphasis on human ability to respond to the gospel and not enough on the grace of God to act in salvation. He achieved a much better balance in maturity.

In the second place, Charles always stressed the work of the Holy Spirit in the use of his revival methods. His main emphasis in this regard was on the "measure" of intercessory prayer. He refused to encourage singing in prayer meeting because it might interrupt the spirit of prayer. Singing in the preaching services, however, was promoted. In Finney's day, revivals tended to be widespread. Many different methods of promoting revival seemed to be blessed. But unlike most evangelists, Charles rarely, if ever, had a dry season in his preaching.

The nature of the new measures hardly seems humanistic to Christians today. Christians now are accustomed to prayer, counseling, and personal witnessing accompanying an evangelistic service as a matter of course.

To some observers, Charles's views on revival seem to be too mechanical, too pat. In effect, he believed that if certain principles were followed, results were sure to come. He compared the process to farming, where sowing, cultivating, and reaping lead to a good crop. Even though the evangelist believed and expounded such ideas, he himself was not mechanical in following them. But others tended to be mechanical, and some of these practices became rote for some of Charles's imitators. The abuse of these practices led to the church's being filled with either evangelistic technicians or confessional theologians. Charles, however, always combined his innovative new measures with a vibrant theology.

Some of the minor issues that Charles was criticized for involved two well-known ministers from New England, the Reverend Lyman Beecher from Boston and the Reverend Asahel Nettleton, a prominent evangelist. Nettleton, nine years older than Charles, had a reputation for being an outstanding revivalist.

The evangelist greatly admired Nettleton and wished to counsel with him as a younger evangelist: "I had the greatest confidence in Mr. Nettleton, though I had never seen him. I felt like sitting at his feet, almost as I would at the feet of an apostle, from what I had heard of his success in promoting revivals. At that time my confidence in him was so great that I think he could have led me, almost or quite, at his discretion."

Charles's desire to sit at Nettleton's feet, however,

was not to be. While Charles was ministering in Troy, Nettleton was holding a revival in Albany. So Charles made the effort to ride over to Albany, hoping to see the older man and hear him preach. He wanted to have Nettleton counsel with him and offer him advice from his position as a more mature evangelist. But Nettleton let Charles know that he did not wish so much as to be seen with him, and Charles had to attend his meeting with another person.

In a letter written on February 15, 1827, Nettleton told Jay Frost: "They [Finney and his friends] are driving us back into barbarism under the illusion of a new era." Later Nettleton wrote to Samuel Aiken: "It is no reflection on his [Finney's] talents or piety, that in his zeal to save souls, he should adopt every measure which promises present success, regardless of consequences; nor, after a fair experiment in so noble a cause, to say, I have pushed something beyond what they will bear, that most useful lessons are learned by experience." Even though Nettleton's tone sounded somewhat conciliatory, he was convinced that Charles should stop using his new measures.

Charles Finney would never do so; he believed that his methods worked, and that they were most useful to bring souls into God's kingdom. Nettleton himself used certain of the new measures, yet criticized Charles for doing so. Most likely he was jealous, to some extent, of the younger evangelist.

For two or three years, the controversy over the new measures raged on. Then on May 27, 1828, when the General Assembly met in Philadelphia, a resolution was passed that finally put it to rest:

The subscribers having had opportunity for free conversation on certain subjects pertaining to revivals of religion, concerning which we have differed, are of the opinion that the general interest of religion would not be promoted by any further publication on those subjects, or personal discussion; and we do hereby engage to cease from all publications, correspondence, conversations, and conduct designed and calculated to keep these subjects before the public's mind; and that, so far as our influence may avail, we will exert it to induce our friends on either side to do the same.

Several well-known church leaders signed the resolution, among them Lyman Beecher and Charles Finney.

The evangelist's life continued to be somewhat tumultuous. He was simply too controversial a figure and accomplished too much for that not to be the case. Nevertheless, Charles retained his new measures to good effect in all the revivals he preached. He determined to put the controversy and criticism behind him and to move forward, turning as many souls to Christ as he could.

ten

As Charles concluded a revival meeting at New Lebanon one Sunday, he encountered Maria, a young woman from nearby Stephentown. She expressed concern for the spiritual well-being of her community and wanted to know if the evangelist would come and preach there. Although moved by her plea, Charles told her that he desired to do so but that he had too many other commitments. Maria's urgent request did cause him to get more information about Stephentown, however.

Charles discovered that Stephentown was north of New Lebanon. He also found out that a strange set of circumstances had caused the town to become spiritually dry. Many years earlier, a wealthy person had died and given the Presbyterian church a fund, the interest from which was sufficient to support a pastor. The pastor who came, however, caused the church to deteriorate and became an infidel, which in turn had a disastrous effect in the town. The entire town had become morally corrupt and spiritually decayed. Such conditions always tantalized Charles, and he felt the pull of the Lord to go there and preach.

A recent New Lebanon convert offered to drive him to Stephentown in his buggy. Charles asked him, "'Have you a steady horse?' The man replied, 'Oh yes! perfectly so,' and smiling, he asked, 'What made you ask the question?' 'Because,' [Charles] responded, 'if the Lord wants me to go to Stephentown, the devil will prevent it if he can; and if you have not a steady horse, he will try to make him kill me.' He smiled, and we rode on; and strange to tell, before we got there, that horse ran away twice, and came near killing us. His owner expressed the greatest astonishment, and said he had never known such a thing before."

The evangelist's arrival in Stephentown generated interest, and he was greeted by a crowd at the designated meeting place. The congregation proved to be solemn and attentive, but nothing of any spiritual significance occurred that Charles could detect, so he did not schedule another meeting. But Maria, the young woman, so plead with him to come back that he finally agreed.

The next Sabbath, the same atmosphere hovered over the meeting, but there seemed to be a more serious attitude in the people. As Charles finished preaching, he took the initiative and set up a third service. He sensed that God was at work after all. During the third service, the Holy Spirit came upon the people—a revival began.

Charles now had to bid farewell to New Lebanon and begin the work in Stephentown. Once he began ministering in earnest, tremendous blessings occurred. Many of the most prominent men in the community were overcome by the power of God.

In an early message, Charles had used as his text, "God is love." A well-to-do farmer attended the service, whom Charles described as "a man of strong nerves, and of considerable prominence as a farmer in the town." The evangelist later recounted: "He sat almost immediately before me, near the pulpit. The first that I observed was that he fell, and writhed in agony for a few moments; but afterwards became still, and nearly motionless, but entirely helpless. He remained in this state until the meeting was out, when he was taken home. He was very soon converted, and became an effective worker in bringing his friends to Christ." Such occurrences often accompanied other revivalists' meetings, as well as Charles's, and they generally had a tremendous effect on the people present.

The evangelist noted: "I have seldom labored in a revival with greater comfort to myself, or with less opposition, than in Stephentown. There was such power set home by the Holy Spirit, that I soon heard no more complaints."

With the "new measures" controversy now behind him, Charles found new joy in his work. While the evangelist had still been in New Lebanon, the Reverend Mr. Gilbert, pastor of the Presbyterian Church in Wilmington, Delaware, had visited him. Although Gilbert was a pastor of "old school" Calvinism, Charles considered him a fine, devout Christian with an earnest desire for people to come to Christ. Even though the two men had theological differences, Gilbert's desire to see sinners come to Christ smoothed the path between them. Further, Gilbert greatly desired Charles to leave Oneida County and come south to Delaware. When he finished at Stephentown, Charles planned to proceed to Delaware.

As the ministry started in Wilmington, however, a new situation confronted Charles: "[Gilbert's] teaching had placed the church in a position that rendered it impossible to promote a revival among them, till their views could be corrected. They seemed to be afraid to make any effort, lest they should take the work out of the hands of God. They had the oldest of the old-school views of doctrine; and consequently their theory was that God would convert sinners in His own time; and that therefore to urge them to immediate repentance, and in short to attempt to promote a revival, was to attempt to make men Christians by human agency, and human strength, and thus to dishonor God by taking the work out of His hands." Charles refused to be discouraged by the situation and decided to try to persuade the Reverend Gilbert to change his mind, so that he could in turn teach his congregation.

After a few weeks of labor and considerable discussion, Charles felt the time had come for the people to hear a thundering "new school" theology sermon. So the following Sabbath he took as his text: "Make you a new heart and a new spirit: for why will ye die?" (Ezekiel 18:31). The evangelist described the sermon with these words: "I went thoroughly into the subject of the sinner's responsibility; and showed what a new heart is not, and what it is. I preached about two hours; and did not sit down till I had gone as thoroughly over the whole subject, as very rapid speaking would enable me to do, in that length of time."

When he finished, Charles met a mixed reaction from the people: Some laughed, some cried, and some were furious. A bewildering turmoil held sway over the congregation. According to the evangelist, "Mr. Gilbert moved himself from one end of the sofa to the other, in the pulpit behind me. I could hear him breathe and sigh, and could not help observing that he was himself in the greatest anxiety. However, I knew I had him, in his convictions, fast; but whether he would make up his mind to withstand what would be said by his people, I did not know. But I was preaching to please the Lord, and not man. I thought that it might be the last time I should ever preach there; but purposed, at all events, to tell them the truth, and the whole truth, on that subject, whatever the result might be."

What Charles desired to show the congregation was that if man were as helpless as they had been taught, he was not to blame for his sins. If he had lost in Adam all ability to obey, and if this had happened not by his own act or consent but by the act of Adam, it was nonsense to say that he could be blamed for what he could not help.

Charles said, "I had endeavored also to show that, in that case, the atonement was no grace, but really a debt due to mankind, on the part of God, for having placed them in a condition so deplorable and so unfortunate. Indeed, the Lord helped me to show up, I think with irresistible clearness the peculiar dogmas of old-schoolism and their inevitable results."

As Charles descended from the pulpit, the people

seemed to be leaving very slowly, and many of them appeared to be waiting for a further word. However, Mrs. Gilbert, the preacher's wife, left immediately. Two ladies standing near the pulpit looked partly grieved, partly offended, and greatly astonished. The first woman the evangelist and the Reverend Gilbert came to took hold of Mr. Gilbert as he was following after Charles. She spoke in a rather loud whisper, "Mr. Gilbert, what do you think of that?"

He replied, "It is worth five hundred dollars." The woman replied, "Then you have never preached the gospel." Gilbert responded, "Well, I am sorry to say I never have." The evangelist was pleased at these remarks; however, when he reached the Gilberts' house, Mrs. Gilbert accosted him about the message, telling him she took exception to what he had preached.

Mrs. Gilbert sensed that the evangelist might be right. She secluded herself in her room for two whole days and emerged not only transformed in theology, but in life as well. Joy beamed from her face. From then on, the work went forward. As for the Reverend Gilbert, his views greatly changed along with his style of preaching and his way of presenting the gospel.

In the meantime, Charles had accepted an invitation to preach in the growing city of Philadelphia twice a week. For a short time, he divided his time between Wilmington and Philadelphia—a distance of about forty miles. As the work in Philadelphia progressed, however, he sensed that he needed to put all of his time in there. So he and Lydia moved to Philadelphia.

From the beginning, Charles's work in Philadelphia took "strong hold." The pastor, the Reverend James Patterson, held views similar to the Reverend Gilbert. But he was a godly man and cared a great deal more for souls than for nice questions about ability and inability, or any of the points of doctrine upon which the old and new school Presbyterians differed. Charles considered the Reverend Patterson "one of the truest and holiest men that I have ever laboured with."

When the Reverend Patterson's wife would say after a good sermon, "Now you see Mr. Patterson, that Mr. Finney does not agree with you on these points upon which we have so often conversed," the minister would reply, "Well, the Lord blesses it." How Charles rejoiced to hear comments like these!

A new and unusual experience opened up for Charles in Philadelphia. The city was much larger than any place he had preached in before, and there were several Presbyterian congregations in the city. So the evangelist was able to rotate his preaching among different churches.

Nearly all the Philadelphia pastors were "old school" men. Patterson was concerned that if the ministers of these churches realized Charles's doctrinal position, they would reject his ministry. But that did not happen. The evangelist found himself accepted in every church except one, the old Arch Street Church.

Charles was never one to modify his views nor his preaching to please people. When he preached in the Arch Street Church, he chose the topic, "There is one God, and one mediator between God and men, the man Christ Jesus" (1 Timothy 2:5). The message struck home to the people's hearts. Invitations flooded in from all over to repeat the message. The evangelist never held back what he believed. As he said, "I felt it my duty to expose all the hiding places of sinners, and to hunt them out from under those peculiar views of orthodoxy, in which I found them entrenched."

In Philadelphia, Charles realized how entrenched the ministers and their people were in "old school" theology —the theology of Princeton Calvinism. The evangelist would later lament, "Where Princeton views were almost universally embraced. . .the greatest difficulty I met with in promoting revivals of religion was the false instruction given to the people, and especially to inquiring sinners. Indeed, in all my ministerial life, in every place and country where I have labored, I have found this difficulty to a greater or less extent; and I am satisfied that multitudes are living in sin, who would immediately be converted if they were truly instructed."

Continuing to point out the difficulty with this doctrine, Charles added, "The foundation of the error of which I speak, is the dogma that human nature is sinful in itself; and that, therefore, sinners are entirely unable to become Christians. It is admitted, expressly or virtually, that sinners may want to be Christians, and that they really do want to be Christians, and often try to be Christians, and yet somehow fail."

Further, Charles pointed out:

It had been the practice, and still is to some extent, when ministers were preaching repentance, and urging the people to repent, to save

*their orthodoxy by telling them that they could not
repent, any more than they could make a world.
But the sinner must be set to do something; and
with all their orthodoxy, they could not bear to
tell him that he had nothing to do. They must
therefore, set him self- righteously to pray for a
new heart. They would sometimes tell him to do
his duty, to press forward in duty, to read his
Bible, to use the means of grace; in short, they
would tell him to do anything and everything, but
the very thing which God commands him to do.
God commands him to repent now, to believe
now, to make to him a new heart now. But they
were afraid to urge God's claims in this form,
because they were continually telling the sinner
that he had no ability whatever to do these things.*

The evangelist used a minister as an example of the theological dilemma. The minister preached a sermon, giving as his text: "Repent and be converted, that your sins
may be blotted out, when the times of refreshing shall
come from the presence of the Lord." The minister,
according to Charles, presented repentance as an invol-
untary change; it consisted simply of being in a state of
sorrow for sin. The minister felt obligated to remind his
congregation that they could not repent; that although
God required it of them, still he knew that it was impossible for them to repent on their own. They could only
repent when God gave them repentance.

The minister concluded his message by telling the
people: "You ask, then, what you shall do. Go home, and

pray for repentance; and if it does not come, pray again for repentance; and still if it does not come, keep praying till it does comes."

When Charles heard this message, he was grieved because he knew the people needed simply to repent by means of their own will. He maintained that the church had things backward: "The church, to a great extent, have instructed sinners to begin on the outside of religion; and by what they have called an outward performance of duty, to secure an inward change of their will and affections." He saw the inclination toward passivity as the stumbling block to people becoming Christians.

In spite of such obstacles, revival winds were blowing through Philadelphia, and before long, Charles realized that going from church to church was not the most satisfactory way to preach. So the evangelist and his co-workers secured a large German church that could hold at least three thousand people, and Charles began to preach nightly. Each night the church filled up with eager listeners; even the aisles filled to capacity. Soon, converts from the revival seemed to be everywhere—not only in the city itself, but in outlying areas as well. For several months, the German church remained home base for the evangelist.

Charles related one of the interesting incidents that took place at the meetings: "There were some cases of very bitter opposition on the part of individuals. In one case, a man whose wife was very deeply convicted, was so enraged that he came in, and took his wife out of the meeting by force. Another case I recollect as a very striking one, of a German whose name I cannot recall. He was a tobacconist. He had a very amiable and intelligent wife;

and was himself, as I afterwards found, when I became acquainted with him, an intelligent man. He was, however, a skeptic, and had no confidence in religion at all. His wife, however, came to our meetings, and became very much concerned about her soul; and after a severe struggle of many days, she was thoroughly converted."

Another incident happened in the spring of 1829. At the time of the spring thaw when the snow and ice melted, the Delaware River was high, and lumbermen floated down the river on homemade rafts. The river ran through Philadelphia, so the men would take their rafts apart and sell the wood for profit. The area these men were from was known as the Lumber Region, an area roughly eighty miles long.

In 1829, the Lumber Region was a complete wilderness, lacking schools, churches, or other community buildings. A number of the lumbermen arriving in Philadelphia that spring came to Charles's revival and became Christians. When they returned home, they prayed diligently for an outpouring of the Holy Spirit. As the new converts shared their faith with their friends and families, they, too, were converted. In a short time, revival broke out in the Lumber Region. The revival spread over the whole area— even to remote places. Some of the people converted had never attended any meetings, and as Charles remarked, were "almost as ignorant as heathens." People even found the Lord in isolated places in the woods.

A man was living alone in the wilderness. Coming under conviction, he sensed that he was alienated from God and became burdened by his sin. He got on his knees, confessed his sin, and asked Christ to become his Savior. The man had never gone to a prayer meeting nor heard a prayer in his life. After he became a Christian, the man shared his new faith with some friends who also lived in the wilderness. They, too, became Christians.

The revival movement continued in these remote areas with hardly any ministers to support it. The movement contained no fanatical elements as was sometimes the case. It was truly a work of God's Holy Spirit. Charles described the wilderness revival "as one of the most remarkable revivals that have occurred in this country."

A singular honor that came to Charles during this time was an invitation to preach at the General Assembly of the Presbytery when it met in Philadelphia. A good friend of the evangelist, John Frost, cautioned him about this opportunity: "Brother Finney, I have said before, keep humble; I repeat it. Don't think more highly of yourself than you ought." Charles's confidence in himself and in the Lord could have been misunderstood as pride, but, above all, he depended totally on the Holy Spirit to carry out God's work through him.

The evangelist remained in Philadelphia for a year and a half. During that time, the city played host to a tremendous revival, and Charles had been catapulted into the limelight. He was now much better known, and no longer had to spend so much energy dealing with controversies such as the old conflict over his "new measures." God was expanding the ministry He had for Charles Finney.

At last, the evangelist's Philadelphia revival had concluded, and he felt drawn to the young, burgeoning city of Reading, Pennsylvania. When Charles arrived in the winter of 1829–30, Reading boasted a population of ten thousand people. Charles was willing to go wherever God sent him, but he sensed that probably his days of preaching in small villages were a thing of the past.

He had been summoned to Reading by Dr. Greer, pastor of the only Presbyterian church in the city. The problems the evangelist encountered in Reading turned out to be somewhat different than those he had in other places. As Charles began to preach in Reading, he quickly discovered that neither the pastor nor the people had any understanding of what a revival was—or even that they needed one. In addition, the people were more interested in dancing and parties than in their spiritual well-being. The evangelist was hard-pressed to get effective prayer meetings started.

With the pastor's approval, Charles preached only to the church members for three weeks. His strongest opponents turned out to be the local reporters who constantly wrote articles criticizing the evangelist and the meetings. But the evangelist-lawyer with his strong, clear logic soon got the better of them, and they stopped printing the articles.

On the third Sunday he preached, Charles sensed that conviction had begun to set in with the people, so he told them he would hold an inquiry meeting. Dr. Greer gave his approval, but he did not think many would attend. Charles mentioned to the people the type of person he thought would come to the meeting; then he invited those individuals who "were seriously impressed with the state of their souls, and had made up their minds to attend immediately to the subject, and desired to receive instruction on the particular question of what they should do to be saved."

The day of the scheduled meeting turned out to be a cold, snowy Monday, yet that evening when Charles and Dr. Greer arrived at the meeting place, they were surprised to see most of the congregation waiting for them. Much to Dr. Greer's amazement, many of the respectable, influential members of his church had decided to attend. The pastor opened the meeting, then turned it over to the evangelist. He explained to Charles, "I know nothing about such a meeting as this; take it into your own hands, and manage it in your own way."

With that, Charles spoke to each person individually and to the group as a whole. He told them he wanted all of them to tell him what they understood about salvation, what their convictions were, and what their difficulties were.

Charles also said to them: "If you were sick and called a physician, he would wish to know your symptoms, and that you should tell him how you were, and how you had been. I cannot adapt instruction to your present state of mind, unless you reveal it to me. The thing, therefore, that I want, is that you reveal, in as few words as you can, your exact state of mind at the present time. I will now pass around among you and give each of you an opportunity to say, in the fewest words, what your state of mind is."

Dr. Greer stayed close to the evangelist as he talked to the people but did not say anything. Charles spoke in a low voice to each one so as not to be overheard by others. He discovered as he moved through the group that there was "a great deal of conviction and feeling in the meeting. They were greatly pressed with conviction. Conviction had taken hold of all classes, the high and the low, the rich and the poor."

Dr. Greer was greatly moved to see his congregation in such a state. He had never had any idea that a penitential state such as he was witnessing could exist. Charles, watching him, thought at times that the pastor was moved nearly to tears.

After speaking with each individual, the evangelist went back to the front of the room and spoke to the group. He shared with them the different situations he had just discovered without revealing any names. Then he tried to clarify all erroneous thinking and suggest ways to overcome their spiritual problems. Above all, Charles wanted to correct their misapprehensions that they must simply wait for God to convert them.

When he had prayed with them, Charles "called on those that felt prepared to submit, and who were willing then and there to pledge themselves to live wholly to God, who were willing to commit themselves to the sovereign mercy of God in Christ Jesus, who were willing to give up all sin, and to renounce it forever, to kneel down, and while I prayed, commit themselves to Christ, and inwardly to do what I exhorted them to do. I called on those only to kneel down, who were willing to do what God required of them, and what I presented before them. Dr. Greer looked very much surprised at the test I put, and the manner in which I pressed them to instant submission."

Following this exhortation, Charles asked those people who wished to, "to kneel, and knelt myself. Dr. Greer knelt by my side, but said nothing. I presented the case in prayer to God, and held right to the point of now submitting, believing, and consecrating themselves to God. There was an awful solemnity pervading the congregation, and the stillness of death, with the exception of my own voice in prayer, and the sobs, and sighs, and weeping that were heard more or less throughout the congregation."

After the prayer of committal, Charles said nothing further and dismissed the group. When Dr. Greer left, he took Charles's hand, saying, "I will see you in the morning."

At about eleven o'clock that same night, a man ran to the evangelist's quarters, called him, and told him that Dr. Greer was dead. When Charles asked what happened, the man told him that Greer had just gone to bed, was taken with "a fit of apoplexy," and died immediately. The pastor's death put a damper on the evangelist's work. But within three weeks or so, the revival once again began to go forward in a powerful way, and many people found Christ as their Savior.

There were many interesting incidents connected with the Reading revival. One of them occurred when at about midnight on a very snowy night, family members knocked on Charles's door, asking him to go out and visit a man who was under such "awful conviction that he could not live unless something was done for him. The man was a stalwart man, very muscular, a man of great force of will and strength of nerve, physically a fine specimen of humanity. His wife was a professor of religion; but he had 'cared for none of these things.' "

The man had attended the meeting earlier that evening, and the sermon had greatly distressed him. Charles added, "He went home in a terrible state of mind, his convictions and distress increasing till it overcame his bodily strength; and his family feared he would die. Despite the stormy night, as we approached the house, I heard his moanings, or rather howlings, before I got near the house. When I entered I found him sitting on the floor, his wife, I believe, supporting his head—and what a look in his face! It was indescribable. Accustomed as I was to seeing persons under great convictions, I must confess that his appearance gave me a tremendous shock. He was writhing in agony, grinding his teeth, and literally gnawing his tongue for pain. He cried out to me, 'O, Mr. Finney! I am lost! I am a lost soul!' I was greatly shocked and exclaimed, 'If this is conviction, what is hell?' "

Charles sat down beside the man and explained salvation in Christ. After talking with the man a short time, Charles led him to accept Christ as his Savior. The man "came out free and joyful in hope."

Another unusual situation that the evangelist encountered had to do with a lawyer who came to see him early one morning. When the man, who belonged to one of the most respectable families in town, called at Charles's room, he was greatly agitated. The man was highly intelligent and a gentleman—but the evangelist could not recall having seen him before. The man then proceeded to tell Charles that he was a lost sinner, and that he had made up his mind there was no hope for him.

Further, he told Charles that when he was at Princeton College, he and two of his classmates became very anxious about their souls. They had gone to talk with Dr. Ashbel Green, then the president of Princeton, and asked him what they should do to be saved. The doctor told them he was glad to have them come and make inquiry. Then he said they should keep out of all bad company, read their Bible regularly, and pray for God to give them a new heart. The president added, "Continue this, and press forward in duty; and the Spirit of God will convert you; or else He will leave you, and you will return back to your sins again."

When the man finished his story, Charles asked him: "'Well, how did it terminate?' 'O,' he said, 'we did just as he told us to do. We kept out of bad company, and prayed that God would make us a new heart. But after a little while our convictions wore away, and we did not care to pray any longer. We lost all interest in the subject.' With that, the young man burst into tears and said, 'My two companions are in drunkards' graves, and if I cannot repent I shall soon be in one myself.'"

Charles said, "I tried to instruct him, and to show him the error that he had fallen into, under such instructions as he had received, and that he had resisted and grieved the Spirit, by waiting for God to do what He had commanded him to do. I tried to show him that, in the very nature of the case, God could not do for him what He required him to do. God required him to repent, and God could not repent for him; required him to believe, but God could not believe for him; God required him to submit, but could not submit for him. I then tried to make him understand the agency that the Spirit of God has in giving the sinner repentance and a new heart; that it is a divine persuasion; that the Spirit leads him to see his sins, urges him to give them up, and to flee from the wrath to come. He presents to him the Savior, the atonement, the plan of salvation, and urges him to accept it."

Then Charles asked the man if he did not feel this urgency of the Spirit upon him, and even a call to submit, to believe, to make himself a new heart. The man cried out fervently that he did see and feel all of it, but wondered even so, if God had not given him up. He asked, "Is not my day of grace past?" The evangelist assured him that the very fact that he had concern for his soul and had come to him showed that the Spirit of God was drawing him, and that it was a divine call. With that, Charles asked him to kneel down, submit to God, and lay hold on eternal life. The man did so and soon rejoiced that he knew Christ as his Savior.

The work in Reading was not easy, but Charles worked long and hard to finish the task God had set before him. In the late spring of 1830, Charles went to Lancaster, Pennsylvania. He found the Presbyterian church there without a pastor, and a dismal spiritual life pervaded the community. After a short time, Charles felt his work in Lancaster was done. As he said, "The work of God was immediately revived, the Spirit of God being poured out almost at once upon the people."

Soon after the Lancaster meetings, the evangelist traveled to New York to visit his father-in-law. While there, he received an invitation to preach as the state legislature was in session in Albany. To be asked to speak to members of the legal profession was a high honor and spoke of Charles's increasing stature.

Sometime later, the evangelist was asked to preach at Old Light Church in New York City. Several of his good friends warned him, however, that it might not be a fruitful time for him. Even Pastor Gale felt that any large city was no place to seek a revival and cautioned Charles that he might lose his evangelistic zeal. But while in New York City, Charles took the opportunity to visit Pough-keepsie, a city about seventy miles north of New York.

The Presbytery session that met in that community resolved: "That we in a Session highly approve to the labors of the Reverend Charles G. Finney among us the past week and do now invite him to return and labor among us as God in His Providence shall open the way."

Another wonderful event took place in New York, too. The Finneys' first son, Charles Beman, was born on March 26, 1830, while the family lived in New York City.

In the summer of 1830, Charles received an invitation to preach in Columbia, New York, a town southeast of Utica. Columbia had a strong German congregation; their large, well-appointed building and numerous members attracted Charles. The situation seemed ideal to him, and he accepted.

But when he arrived in Columbia, Charles learned that all was not as it appeared. The pastor who had invited Charles had trained under a German doctor of divinity who had completely discouraged any form of dynamic religious experience. But the pastor's mother was a devout Christian who had prayed earnestly for her son. When the young man had been called to pastor the Columbia church, his mother had shared with him what Christ can mean in a person's life, and the pastor found Christ.

The pastor then began witnessing to his wife, church members, and the elders, but when he learned that Charles was in New York, he had invited him to preach. When Charles began preaching, he quickly discerned that the church members, though doctrinally orthodox, had not had a personal experience with Jesus Christ. They believed that correct theology was all that was needed to be a good Christian.

Although Charles wondered if revival could ever take root in such a dry place, he faithfully preached God's Word. A revival began which spread throughout the community.

Later, a wealthy philanthropist, Hansan G. Phelps, visited Charles and invited him to come preach in New York City once more. The evangelist did and revival broke out as in other places. He stayed in New York for sometime preaching the gospel.

The New York revival proved to be significant to Charles's ministry. First, it opened the door for the organization of what was then called free Presbyterian churches in the city. Converts of the Finney revival attended these churches. Also, the New York ministry allowed Charles to get to know the Tappan brothers. This contact would be very useful in the evangelist's future ministry. Then, Charles came to understand New York, and in turn, New York became acquainted with the evangelist. This set the stage for even further ministry in America's largest metropolitan area.

Charles's days as a traveling evangelist were fast coming to a close. However, at this point, he received an invitation to go to Rochester, New York. An elder of the Third Presbyterian Church in Rochester had corresponded with the evangelist and shared many of the city's needs. Charles had received other invitations to preach, and he faced a dilemma. Where should he go next? He simply did not know what to do.

Many aspects about a Rochester revival troubled Charles. Leadership in the churches was undergoing change. The Second Presbyterian Church, called the "Brick Church," had a good pastor, but he was leaving. The Reverend Parker, pastor of the Third Presbyterian Church, had left and become a pastor to one of the new free churches in New York City.

Another problem was a controversy that existed between a Third Church elder and the First Presbyterian pastor. Despite these difficulties, certain friends at Rochester continued to try to convince Charles that he should come. Charles had been visiting his father-in-law's home while trying to find God's will. He felt the need for the support of prayerful friends, so Charles and his family packed up and traveled to Utica, where a large number of such friends lived.

The Finney family arrived in Utica in the afternoon, and by night a number of their faithful friends gathered for prayer and consultation. They each expressed their opinions about what Charles should do. All of them agreed that he should not go to Rochester. It was too uninviting to start a revival. They thought he should accept one of the invitations to Philadelphia or New York

City. Those places offered much brighter prospects.

The family went to bed that evening, expecting to take the canal boat to New York City in the morning. But Charles was unable to sleep. He kept asking himself, *Why am I not going to Rochester?* As he mulled over the reasons for his decision, he began to realize that what others saw as detriments were actually the very reasons he should go. He felt ashamed that he had not recognized this sooner. He was avoiding the city because of the difficulties he saw. That night God gave him the assurance that He would go with him and give him wonderful meetings.

Never one to hesitate once he knew God's will, Charles told his family of his decision in the morning. Thus the family began the long trip west to Rochester.

eleven

Charles and his family arrived in Rochester, New York, by canal packet boat on September 10, 1830. Josiah Bissell, the leading elder of the Third Presbyterian Church, met the family at the dock and took them to stay at his home. Elder Bissell was the elder who had a disagreement with Dr. Penny, pastor of the First Presbyterian Church.

Although Charles began preaching almost at once in the Third Presbyterian Church, he had a cousin who attended First Presbyterian Church and who introduced him to the pastor, Dr. Penny. Dr. Penny made it a point to hear Charles preach, and the two men became fast friends.

The conflict between Elder Bissell and Dr. Penny had begun over the calling of a pastor to the Second Presbyterian Church. A strong-willed and, at times, stubborn man, Bissell did not agree with the person Dr. Penny thought should be called. The rift between the two men and the anger it caused had spread through both churches and caused much bitterness. As God's Spirit moved through the city bringing revival, however, the conflict between the men was resolved. Each man took responsibility for his own wrongdoing in the situation.

Not only did Rochester begin to feel the effect of Charles's ministry, but people from outlying places such as Henrietta, Pittsfield, and Canandaiqua did as well. Charles also preached in the surrounding cities of Clarkson, Brock-port, Ogden, and Penfield.

Rochester took great pride in its large number of lawyers, and many of these men came to the meetings and became Christians. They were impressed by Charles's logical, legal style—his clear explanations of the Scriptures and the way of salvation. Not only did numerous lawyers attend the meetings, but people from all walks of life, including businessmen, teachers, and ordinary workers. Charles was amazed at the numbers of people accepting Christ at his meetings. There had never been so many conversions.

A short time after Charles began preaching, it was difficult to find a room large enough to hold the crowds. This problem intensified after an accident that occurred on October 1, early in the revival. In the middle of the service at the First Presbyterian Church, as Dr. Penny was praying, an explosive sound roared through the building. The stone walls started to give way, and with a thunderous crash, a large timber from the ceiling crashed through the plaster and landed in front of the organ.

The scene became pandemonium. People panicked

and started running in every direction. Charles gives a humorous account of the melee: "Before I had time to think again, Dr. Penny leaped from the pulpit almost over me, for I was kneeling by the sofa behind him. The pulpit was in the front of the church, between the two doors. The rear wall of the church stood upon the brink of the canal. The congregation, in a moment, fell into a perfect panic, and rushed for the doors and the windows, as if they were all distracted. One elderly woman held up a window in the rear of the church, where several, as I was informed, leaped out into the canal. The rush was terrific. Some jumped over the galleries into the aisles below, they ran over each other in the aisles."

As people ran every which way, Charles tried to bring order to the chaos: "I stood up in the pulpit, and not knowing what had happened, put up my hands, and cried at the top of my voice, 'Be quiet! Be quiet!' Directly a couple of women rushing up into the pulpit, one on the one side, and the other on the other side, caught hold of me, in a state of distraction. Dr. Penny ran out into the streets, and they were getting out in every direction, as fast as possible. As I did not know that there was any danger, the scene looked so ludicrous to me, that I could scarcely refrain from laughing. They rushed over each other in the aisles, so that in several instances I observed men that had been crushed down, rising up and throwing off others that had rushed upon them. All at length got out. Several were considerably hurt, but no one killed. But the house was strewn with all sorts of women's apparel. Bonnets, shawls, gloves, handkerchiefs, and parts of dresses, were scattered in every direction. The men had generally gone without their hats, I believe."

Since the building was located near the canal, it was later determined that the damp soil surrounding the building had caused the church to settle in obviously dangerous ways. Following the disastrous incident at First Presbyterian Church, a new location had to be found for the meetings. Charles was concerned, as well, that the near-tragedy might mar the spirit of the revival, but fortunately that did not happen. The work went on and continued to increase.

Now the Brick Church opened its doors for the meetings, and once the arrangements had been made, the meetings continued with growing attendance. The evangelist also began alternating the meetings between the various Presbyterian churches. Inquiry meetings and prayer meetings were held in different churches as well. In fact, all denominations began to work together in the revival effort. The revival was spreading beyond the Presbyterian churches.

One of the high schools in Rochester was led by a pastor's son from nearby Brighton. Many of the students began attending the revival services and came under conviction. Sometime later, the school's director found the students unable to recite their lessons for class that day because of their deep consciousness of sin. The director called for one of his associates who was a Christian, and told her that his young people were so concerned for their souls, they were unable to do their schoolwork. In spite of his skepticism, he suggested she send for Charles to come and speak to them. Of course, the evangelist was more than willing to do so. Following his talk to the teenagers, nearly every person in the school was converted—including the skeptical director.

The Rochester revival ushered at least forty men into the gospel ministry. Because of Charles's preaching, they dedicated their lives to the ministry. Of the forty, a number also became foreign missionaries. Rochester also became the first place where Charles used what he termed the "anxious seat." He explained what he believed the anxious seat would accomplish:

> *I had never, I believe, except in rare instances, until I went to Rochester, used as a means of promoting revivals, what has since been called "the anxious seat." I had sometimes asked persons in the congregation to stand up; but this I had not frequently done. However, in studying upon the subject, I had often felt the necessity of some measure that would bring sinners to a stand. From my own experience and observation, I had found that, with the higher classes especially, the greatest obstacle to be overcome was their fear of being known as anxious inquirers. They were too proud to take any position that would reveal them to others as anxious for their souls.*
>
> *I had found also that something was needed, to make the impression on them that they were expected at once to give up their heart; something that would call them to act, and act as publicly before the world, as they had in their sins; something that would commit them publicly to the service of Christ. When I had called them simply to*

stand up in the public congregation, I found that
this had a very good effect; and so far as it went,
it answered the purpose for which it was intended.
But after all, I had felt for some time, that some-
thing more was necessary to bring them out from
among the mass of the ungodly, to a public
renunciation of their sinful ways, and a public
committal of themselves to God.

The anxious seat was another of Charles's new measures, and as he said, he began using it regularly long after the earlier controversies over his new methods of presenting the gospel had been resolved. He constantly sought new and better ways to help people in their commitment to Christ.

The Rochester revivals received a great deal of newspaper coverage, and most of it was quite favorable. At these meetings, the upper classes in intellect, education, and culture, along with average citizens, approved of what they saw and heard. It was a new day for Charles and his ministry. His new stamp of approval was reflected in papers such as the *Rochester Observer,* which stated:

We have never known a revival more general
among all classes, the youth, and those who are
preparing for, and those who have just entered
upon, the great theatre of life—the student, the
mechanic, the professional man, and the politi-
cian —those who were seeking for, and those who
are in possession of office and worldly honors,
have been arrested by the Spirit of God, and a
new song has been put in their mouths.

Other publications also spoke well of Charles and the revivals. One especially glowing account was written by Henry B. Stanton, a lawyer and journalist who exercised great influence over other people's opinions. Stanton declared:

In October, 1830, Charles G. Finney, the famous evangelist, came to Rochester to supply the pulpit of the Third Presbyterian Church. I had been ab-sent a few days and on my return was asked to hear him. It was in the afternoon. A tall, grave-looking man, dressed in an unclerical suit of grey, ascended the pulpit. I listened. It did not sound like preaching, but like a lawyer arguing a case before a court and jury. The discourse was a chain of logic brightened by felicity of illustration and enforced by urgent appeals from a voice of great compass and melody. Mr. Finney was there in the fullness of his power. His style was particularly attractive to law-yers. He illustrated his points frequently and happily by reference to legal principle. It began with the judges, the lawyers, the physicians, the bankers, and the merchants, and worked its way down to the bottom of society, till nearly everybody had joined one or the other of the churches controlled by the different denominations. I have heard many celebrated pulpit orators in various parts of the world. Taking all in all, I have never heard the superior of Charles G. Finney.

Charles had learned his early lessons as a law student well. A supreme court judge had advised him, "Charlie, you win a legal case by telling it simply; repeated as many times as there are men in the box. Tell it simply. And never read it! Have it so well in hand that you can look the jury in the eye and see if you are moving them. If you are not, you will have to change your tactics so that you will move them."

As a result of this good advice, the preacher Finney's speech was colloquial, direct, and pungent. Later, when he became a professor of theology and an instructor of young preachers, Charles would tell them: "What would be thought of a lawyer who should stand up before a jury and read an essay to them? He would lose his case! I talk to the people as I would have talked to a jury."

He chose his illustrations from life more than from classical literature. Thus, his examples were down-to-earth and on a level where people lived their lives. In short, he broke all the conventions of the preaching style of the day, but he communicated in a way that struck home to his listeners' hearts. His preaching was relevant to their lives.

Charles also proved to be a thinker and assumed his hearers were thinkers as well. In the preface to the *Systematic Theology*, he wrote: "My brother, sister, friends—reason, study, think—you were made to think. God designed that religion should require thought; intense thought and should thoroughly develop our powers of thought. The Bible itself is written in the style so condensed as to require much intense study."

One of his contemporaries described the evangelist in

the following way: "As the preacher, he stood at his full height, tall and majestic, stood as if transfixed, gazing and pointing toward the emblazoned cloud, as it seemed to roll up before him; his clear, shrill voice rising to its highest pitch, and penetrating every nook and corner of the vast assembly. People held their breath. Every heart stood still. It was almost enough to raise the dead—and there were no sleepers within the sound of his clarion voice." Someone else said of him: "Why, it didn't seem like preaching. It seemed as if Mr. Finney had taken me alone, and was conversing with me face-to-face."

Another change in the Rochester revival was that, above all, it was a revival with dignity and decorum. No falling in the aisles or shrieks or groanings occurred such as had happened in earlier places like Evans Mills and Gouverneur. The *New York Evangelist* declared about the meetings: "From all that can be learned by private letters, and by oral testimony, . . .that almost every town within forty or fifty miles of Rochester is favoured more or less with the special presence of the Lord."

Charles also said of the revival, "The great majority of the leading men and women of the city were converted." So the Rochester revival was reported as being an outstanding one in every way, changing many of the citizens who, in turn, changed their city.

The Rochester revival played a part in the general Third Great Awakening that swept America during the decade of the 1830s. Even Lyman Beecher gave Charles credit for his role in the revival: "That was the greatest work of God, and the greatest revival of religion, that the world has ever seen in so short a time. One hundred thousand were reported as having connected themselves with churches as the result of that great revival. This is unparalleled in the history of the church, and the progress of religion." Beecher acknowledged that no year during the Christian era had reported such a great revival of religion.

Of course, a general American awakening occurred during the time of the Rochester revival, making the one in Rochester a single aspect of the whole. But Charles Finney played a large part in the far-reaching Rochester revival, and to a great extent, he was credited with its amazing success. Following the end of the Rochester meetings, however, the Finneys would turn in a different direction: New York City. There a new and different kind of ministry awaited them.

twelve

P rior to the Finneys' going to New York City,
however, Charles needed rest. He was physically
exhausted, and several doctors were concerned
that he would never be able to preach again. They even
thought he might have a fatal disease called consumption
(often the term given to what we call tuberculosis).
Charles wanted to prove them wrong and resolutely
decided to continue with his ministry.

As he left for Schenectady, New York, in the spring of
1831, Charles wondered how God would lead him. He
had been invited to preach at Union College in the city,
and would be the guest of Dr. Mott, its president.

En route to the city, Charles decided to stop and rest
at Auburn, and while he waited, a man appeared with a
paper full of signatures urging him to stay and preach. As
he reviewed the names, he was surprised to see many signatures of prominent men, even some who had opposed

him earlier. Profoundly moved, he took the matter to the Lord and was favorably impressed to stay.

Because of his fatigue, however, he set forth certain conditions for his preaching: He would preach twice on Sunday and on two weekly nights. Besides these engagements, he would see no visitors save under extreme circumstances, so he could rest.

The people accepted his conditions thankfully, and Charles began to preach. The evangelist noted of the meetings: "The word took immediate effect." After the message, on his first Sunday ministering, Charles issued an invitation for those who wanted to renounce their sins and receive Christ to come forward publicly declaring their decision. At this point, giving a public invitation to accept Christ was one of the regular new measures that Charles used quite effectively. The first person among numerous others to come forward was the person who led the opposition to Charles earlier during the previous Auburn revival.

Charles preached in Auburn for six weeks, and in that time, roughly five hundred people professed faith in Christ. Charles realized about the revival that: "This revival seems to be only a wave of divine power, reaching Auburn from the center at Rochester, whence such a mighty influence had gone out over the length and breadth of the land." The Rochester revival had continued to have an impact on the surrounding areas of New York. Several years later, a historian of the First Presbyterian Church of Auburn wrote a vivid account of Charles and the work there:

He was then at the prime of life and at the height of his fame. As a preacher, he was without a

161

*rival. The glance of his full sharp eye and the
tones of his commanding voice were in keeping
with the sterner aspects of truth, which he never
failed to present with searching discrimination
and powerful effect. Mr. Finney preached in no
other pulpit than this, but the results were by
no means limited to this congregation. Many,
who ascribe their conversion to his instrumentality, united with other churches in the village and
vicinity; and now, after a generation has passed,
and with it the prejudice of the time, there can be
no question of the service then rendered to the
cause of vital religion.*

Due to the numerous invitations Charles received during his Auburn stay, he decided against going to Union College as he had planned. Instead, he went to Buffalo where he preached for one month. Though his stay in Buffalo was brief, a large number of people were con-verted, including many prominent citizens. Increasingly, the evangelist's revivals encompassed those described as upper-class New Yorkers.

In June, Charles left for his father-in-law's home in Oneida County. He needed time for rest and recreation and to regain strength, so he stayed there most of the summer. Lydia's family certainly didn't object to the opportunity to spend time with their daughter and her growing family. Early autumn found the evangelist min-istering in Providence, Rhode Island, where he stayed just three weeks. He sensed, however, that "my stay was too short to secure so general a work of grace in that place, as occurred afterwards in 1842, when I spent some two months there."

The next place he was invited to preach was Boston. This invitation came as a complete surprise to Charles, but he rose to the challenge. He even preached in Park Street Church where Edward Beecher, Lyman Beecher's son, served as pastor. The Boston believers, however, seemed spiritually cold in response to his first sermon, so the evangelist tried some new tactics. His next sermons were very probing and penetrating.

The tactic seemingly backfired. Charles watched the congregation begin to dwindle. Each night there were fewer and fewer people attending. This was a completely new experience for him. He had never seen Christians "shrink back," as he said. The believers, though, saw things differently. They wondered, "What will the Unitarians say, if such things are true of us who are orthodox? If Mr. Finney preaches to us in this way, the Unitarians will triumph over us, and say, that at least the orthodox are not better Christians than Unitarians."

They felt resentment at Charles's intense probing, so they actively rejected it. As always, however, the Spirit of God began to move in response to prayer, overcoming the believers' objections. The Christians began to listen intensely to Charles's sermons and gradually came to appreciate them. Even Lyman Beecher, Charles's former enemy on the new measures issue, jumped in with enthusiasm. Although he willingly took part in the revival meetings, Pastor Beecher was relieved to leave the inquirers' meetings to Charles. The younger evangelist, always gracious to Beecher, handled the situation with the utmost delicacy so as not to offend nor embarrass him. Overall, the Boston meetings turned out to be quite successful. Finally Charles had gained acceptance in one of the most conservative, traditional cities in America.

At last the evangelist's travels had come to an end, and the Finneys would proceed to a new challenge: filling a church pulpit in New York City.

thirteen

Charles was as surprised as anyone when he received a call to pastor the Second Free Presbyterian Church in New York City. As he made clear: "Having had no training for the ministry, I did not expect nor desire to labor in large towns and cities, nor minister to cultivated communities. I intended to go to the new settlements, and preach in schoolhouses and barns and groves as best I could."

His pulpit in New York, however, was a renovated theater on old Chatham Street. Charles was gratified when, after a brief interval, "the Spirit of the Lord was immediately poured out upon us and we had an extensive revival that spring and summer." At the first service, more than two thousand people packed the theater, and the crowds continued to come regularly after that.

A few months after the evangelist had come to New York, a severe epidemic of cholera broke out. People retreated from the city in droves, hoping to escape the dreaded disease. The Chatham Street section was especially hard hit, and Charles wrote that one morning he counted five hearses at nearby houses, waiting to collect the dead.

With true pastoral concern, Charles stayed in the city with his family so he could minister to the suffering and dying people. After a time, his own strength was depleted, and he went to the country for two weeks of rest. He returned for his installation service as pastor of the Second Free Presbyterian Church.

The service, of course, was a joyous time, but in the middle of it, Charles became very ill. Following the benediction, he went home, got in bed, and called the doctor. The doctor's diagnosis was the one he dreaded. Charles had cholera. His next-door neighbor got cholera the same day, and the following morning the neighbor was dead.

Both the Second Free Presbyterian Church congregation and the doctor gave Charles a stern warning: rest or die. Help was sought to provide Charles with time to convalesce, and an associate pastor, Jacob Heffenstein, arrived to carry on with ministerial duties.

A year or so before this turn of events, when Charles was still recovering from cholera, his doctor had recommended a sea voyage to the Mediterranean to restore his health. So that winter he left by himself on a small ship going east across the Atlantic, which is notorious for stormy weather during that time of year. The little ship tossed violently up and down, and Charles's cabin was anything but comfortable.

Then Charles discovered that the captain was an alcoholic, and on one occasion, during a storm, the captain could not even manage the ship. Incredibly, the command fell to Charles, who had learned sailing years earlier on Lake Ontario. Not only did Charles save the ship but his fellow passengers as well.

Following his sea experience, the evangelist spent a few weeks recuperating on the island of Malta and in Sicily. By the time he left for home, he was almost as exhausted as when he left. But on the way home, Charles had an encounter with God and met Him in a fresh, new way. Of that experience, he says:

On my homeward passage my mind became exceedingly exercised on the question of revivals. I feared that they would decline throughout the country. I feared that the opposition that had been made to them, had grieved the Holy Spirit. My own health, it appeared to me, had nearly or quite broken down; and I knew of no other evangelist that would take the field, and aid pastors in revival work. This view of the subject distressed me so much that one day I found myself unable to rest. My soul was in an utter agony. I spent almost the entire day in prayer in my stateroom, or walking the deck in such agony as to wring my hands and almost to gnaw my tongue, as it were, in view of the state of things. In fact, I felt crushed with the burden that was on my soul. There was no one on board to whom I could open my mind, or say a word.

It was the spirit of prayer that was upon me; that which I had often experienced in kind, but perhaps never before to such a degree, for so long a time. I besought the Lord to go on with His work, and to provide Himself with such instrumentalities as were necessary. It was a long summer day, in the early part of July. After a day of unspeakable wrestling and agony in my soul, just at night, the subject cleared up to my mind. The Spirit led me to believe that all would come out right, and that God had yet a work for me to do; that I might be at rest; that the Lord would go forward with His work; and give me strength to take any part in it that He de-sired. But I had not the least idea what the course of His providence would be.

While Charles was overseas, the members of Chatham Street Church, along with a group of abolitionists, held a liberation rally on July 4, but the meeting stirred up some enemies. The anti-abolitionists thought it was an anti-slavery rally, and the entire event grew out of proportion.

Returning from his voyage, Charles was met by the Reverend Joshua Leavitt, the editor of the *New York Evangelist,* a publication which supported Finney's new measures. The periodical had been created as a voice in opposition to *The Observer,* a publication partial to Asahel Nettleton. Earlier, *The Observer* had refused to print anything favorable to Charles, so the evangelist's friends had started the other periodical. Now Leavitt gave Charles some stunning news. Being a fervent abolitionist, Leavitt had fired off tirades in the *Evangelist* opposing slavery. The result was that they had lost many subscribers and the subscriber list was now dangerously small.

In a voice choking with emotion, Leavitt told Charles: "Brother Finney, I have ruined the *Evangelist*. I have not been prudent as you cautioned me to be, and I have gone so far ahead of public intelligence and feeling on the subject [of abolition], that my subscription list is rapidly failing; and we shall not be able to continue its publication beyond the first of January, unless you can do something to bring the paper back to public favor again." Sadly, Charles responded that his health would not permit him to do much.

Then Leavitt told him that if he could write a series of articles on revivals, he believed that the paper could be restored to public favor. Charles tossed the idea around for a couple days and then gave his answer to the editor. He said that he would preach an entire course of revival lectures to his church, which could then be published in the *Evangelist*. Leavitt was ecstatic. In the following issue of the paper, he advertised the forthcoming series, and the subscriptions increased almost immediately. He boasted to Charles: "I have as many new subscribers every day, as would fill my arms with papers."

Through the winter of 1834 and 1835, the evangelist gave one lecture each week on revival. Leavitt recorded the gist of Charles's message in longhand, and the next day, he filled in his sketchy notes as best he could. The evangelist never edited nor developed the articles in any way, and they went directly to press from Leavitt's hand.

Charles's oral messages lasted about one and a half hours; Leavitt's recorded notes on the lectures can be read in roughly one-third of that time.

The interest sparked by Charles's lecture series was phenomenal. Each Friday night the building overflowed with eager listeners. Not only did the series on revival save the *Evangelist*, it soon found its way into book form under the title, *Lectures on Revivals of Religion*. Thus was born a revivalistic classic. Twelve thousand copies sold initially, but as fast as the press could produce new editions, they were sold out. Soon, they were translated into French, German, and Welsh. The English bought tens of thousands of editions, as did the entire English-speaking world. Even though the recorded messages left out much, the lectures have become timeless.

Perhaps the lectures' most amazing impact was the revivals it birthed for years to come. In Merioneth, Wales, revival broke out in 1840. The book also promoted many conversions in England and Scotland, and numerous young men were called into the ministry. The views of William and Catherine Booth, who later founded the Salvation Army, were greatly influenced by Charles's *Lectures on Revivals*. The book stirred people all over America, as well, with its clarion call to revival.

Charles refused to take credit for the book. He saw the book as a spiritual victory:

This was not of man's wisdom. Let the reader remember that long day of agony and prayer at sea, that God would do something to forward the

170

*work of revivals, and enable me, if He desired to
do it, to take such a course as to help forward the
work. I felt certain then that my prayers would be
answered; and I have regarded all that I have
since been able to accomplish, as in a very
important sense, an answer to the prayers of
that day. The spirit of prayer came upon me as
a sovereign grace, bestowed upon me without the
least merit, and in spite of all my sinfulness, He
pressed my soul in prayer, until I was enabled to
prevail; and through the infinite riches of grace
in Christ Jesus, I have been many years witnessing the wonderful results of that day of wrestling
with God. In answer to that day's agony, He has
continued to give me the spirit of prayer.*

In spite of the success of the printed lectures, Charles had
concerns about his congregation when he returned to the
pulpit, after nearly a year of convalescence. He attempted
to bring revival to the church, however, in his own words,
"Very little was accomplished." New York City was different from the other places he had preached. He would
have to discover new ways to reach the city's people.

With renewed determination, Charles began a program
of nightly preaching at the church following his basic revival philosophy. Almost immediately, a tremendous revival
began, and during twenty days of preaching, more than
five hundred conversions were recorded. In addition, the
church itself added so many members that another church,
or colony, as Charles called it, was formed.

The preacher of the Second Free Presbyterian Church

also proved popular with many different types of people, including young people. With his reasoned sermons and teaching, Charles helped young people to gain confidence in their faith.

Some time later, a woman came into the church who had committed an offense in another New York Presbyterian church. In accordance with a previous ruling, the Chatham Street Church excommunicated her. She then appealed to the presbytery, and the presbytery acquitted her. The presbytery also took Chatham Street Church to task for their action. With that decision, Charles and the presbytery began a debate, and Dr. Cox of the presbytery spoke vehemently against the evangelist and Chatham Church. Soon, this incident stirred up the old controversy over Charles's new measures.

Shortly after the discipline debate came to a boil, some Christian lay people decided to build a large new church on Broadway. The people wanted two things: a Congregational church and Charles Finney as their pastor. Of course, there were many Congregational ministers they could have called, but there was only one Finney. Would he be willing to leave his Presbyterian ties and come minister to them?

Charles later said nothing of the anguish his decision must have caused him, but simply reported: "I then took my dismission from the presbytery, and became pastor of that Congregational church." The Broadway Church would turn out to be Charles's most commanding platform.

The building of the Broadway Church was not without controversy. Rumors began to fly that the new church building on Broadway would be a center of abolitionist sentiment. While the building was still under construction, someone set fire to it. Feelings were so intense over the issue that the local fire brigade refused to put the fire out. The entire interior and the roof were demolished. Only the walls were left standing.

Though fire had partially destroyed the Broadway Church, construction began anew, and it was finished in a relatively short time. Charles himself designed the building, over the architect's objections. The evangelist told him, in effect, "If you won't follow my design, I'll get someone who will." The finished product suited Charles just fine: "It was a most commodious and comfortable place to speak in."

Just before Charles would resume preaching in the Broadway Church, several young men asked him if he would tutor them as students in theology. He declined, stating that he had his hands full with pastoring a church. Nevertheless, the request began to plague the evangelist.

The students continued to badger him on this issue, and soon, applications poured in for a series of theological messages. Charles finally decided to deliver a whole series of lectures on the basic theological concepts of the Christian faith; students could come as they desired.

About the same time as the theological series was being given, John J. Shipherd and Philo P. Stewart founded a small school in northern Ohio named Oberlin Collegiate Institute. The school's charter was granted in February 1834. The institute was located about thirty-three miles west of Cleveland on a wooded five-hundred-acre plot. The school was named for John Frederick Oberlin, a distinguished French pastor from Alsace in the Vosges Mountains in France. Oberlin had achieved renown as a Christian philanthropist.

In January 1835, after Charles had started the theological lectures at Broadway Church, John Shipherd and Asa Mahan of Cincinnati approached him. They had come to ask Theodore Weld to be Oberlin's professor of theology, but Weld had declined. He recommended Charles Finney as the only man for the post. Now the two men put their proposition before the evangelist.

After much prayer, Charles decided he could divide his time and efforts between the Broadway Tabernacle and the Oberlin Institute. He would spend the six winter months in New York and then travel to Oberlin to spend the six summer months at the school. The Oberlin trustees approved the appointment of Charles by an overwhelming margin. Some of the stipulations that Charles put forth before he agreed to the post included: (1) the trustees must agree not to get involved in the internal affairs of the school, and (2) no one should be denied admission on the basis of race or sex—black students should be admitted on the same basis as white, and women should be admitted on the same basis as men.

Some of the trustees objected to this last point, but Charles, Shipherd, Mahan, and others stood firm, and the condition was granted. Oberlin Institute became the first co-educational college in the history of American higher education. It was also one of the first institutions to accept students regardless of race or color.

Charles prepared to move his family to Oberlin in the early summer of 1835. He was reluctant to leave his pastorate but knew that God had called him to go to Ohio. For some time the dual role of pastor and professor proved successful. But as his responsibilities grew, Charles knew he would have to choose between the two posts.

He resigned the pastorate of the New York church in April 1837. The congregation wrote him a note of thanks: "We gratefully acknowledge the goodness of God in so greatly blessing the labors of our pastor among us— while we bow with humble resignation with that Divine Providence which has brought us to the painful necessity of separation."

Although he hated to leave his church, Charles knew his calling was to prepare young men for the ministry. Such an undertaking could best be accomplished in his new position. He would be able to instruct and teach his students what he had already learned. As a full-time theological professor, Charles would be training men to do what he had done so well—be an evangelist for God.

fourteen

Greeting the Finneys as they arrived in Oberlin, Ohio, in 1835, was a huge three-thousand-seat tent with a lofty banner fluttering over it announcing, "Holiness to the Lord." The tent, a token of love and appreciation to Charles, came by way of his band of friends and admirers. Now he would be able to hold revival services on the Oberlin campus in addition to fulfilling his new responsibilities as professor of theology. A short time later, the Oberlin Congregational Church was formed, and Charles was selected to be pastor. He held that position for years to come.

At the time the Finney family arrived, not many Oberlin campus buildings had been built. Once Charles's friends learned of his new commitment at Oberlin, however, many of them rallied to help the fledgling institute. Several close friends and associates of the evangelist also became part of Oberlin's select faculty. These included

Asa Mahan, Oberlin's first president; John Morgan, professor of New Testament language and literature (he and Charles labored together in Oberlin's revival services); Henry Cowles, professor of Greek and Latin; and his wife, Alice Welch Cowles, who served as principal of the Oberlin Female Department.

Oberlin's organization consisted of two academic disciplines: the liberal arts college and the theological seminary. Moreover, religion encompassed each area of study. Charles summed up Oberlin's philosophy when he spoke to the 1851 graduating class: "You are not only educated, but educated in God's college—a college reared under God, and for God, by the faith, the prayers, the toils, and the sacrifices of God's people. You cannot but know that it has been the sole purpose of the founders and patrons of this college to educate you men and women for God and for God's cause." Oberlin's solid foundation on strong Christian principles helped the school get off to a good start.

The initial student body consisted of one hundred students, and many of them did manual labor in exchange for their tuition. They could work on the school farm and other buildings to earn the money they needed. But the trustees also believed it was profitable for the students to develop good health and keep in physical condition. When a severe financial crisis hit Oberlin in the early years, the student work program turned out to be a tremendous help.

Shortly after the campus building program got under way, Arthur Tappan, who backed the school financially, suffered a devastating business loss from fire. Following that blow, the nation experienced an economic recession, so Tappan had to declare bankruptcy. Probably Charles wondered in those early days whether he had done the right thing leaving a secure, successful pastorate for college life in the American wilderness.

Soon after the family's arrival in Oberlin, Charles learned that his *Lectures on Revivals of Religion* had reached England and received much acclaim. He also knew that the British Christian public would appreciate Oberlin Institute's stance on abolition, collegiate co-education, and social reform, so he suggested that John Keep and William Dawes be sent to England to do some fund-raising. The English did respond, and the men returned with six thousand pounds.

Other American Christians pitched in, too, to help the struggling school. Some of the people from Ohio, however, were opposed to the college's abolitionist stand and refused to help. There was even talk by the state legislature of Ohio about rescinding the college charter. The school overcame all these difficulties in time as Christians on both sides of the Atlantic gave generously to the institute.

Charles and his family suffered financially during these times, but he knew God would provide for them. He later recalled an example of just how the Lord provided for his family's needs:

> *At one time, I saw no means of providing for my family through the winter. Thanksgiving day came, and found us so poor that I had been obliged to sell my traveling trunk, which I had used in my*

evangelistic labors, to supply the place of a cow which I had lost. I rose on the morning of Thanksgiving, and spread our necessities before the Lord. I finally concluded by saying that, if help did not come, I should assume that it was best that it should not; and would be entirely satisfied with any course that the Lord would see it wise to take. I went and preached, and enjoyed my own preaching as well, I think, as I ever did. I had a blessed day in my own soul; and I could see that the people enjoyed it exceedingly.

After the meeting, I was detained a little while in conversation with some brethren, and my wife returned home. When I reached the gate, she was standing in the open door, with a letter in her hand. As I approached she smilingly said, "The answer has come, my dear"; and handed me the letter containing a cheque from Mr. Josiah Chapin of Providence, for two hundred dollars. He had been here the previous summer, with his wife. I had said nothing about my wants at all, as I never was in the habit of mentioning them to anybody. But in the letter containing the cheque, he said he had learned that the endowment fund had failed, and that I was in want of help. He intimated that I might expect more, from time to time. He continued to send six hundred dollars a year, for several years; and on this I managed to live.

Despite the hardships Charles and his family endured, he

always tried to be generous to others. Hearing about a missionary to the Ojibway Indians who had no overcoat, Charles gladly sent him the best one he had. It had cost him about fifty dollars, a considerable amount of money in the nineteenth century. The Oberlin Institute might not have continued had it not been for Charles and his followers, who always gave largely to the school.

Charles also seemed to have a penchant for getting into trouble with other church leaders. During the years when he divided his time between New York and Oberlin, the evangelist (along with Asa Mahan) had worked out his concepts of perfectionism and sanctification. Charles called the series "Lectures to Professing Christians." The lectures first appeared in Leavitt's *New York Evangelist,* then went into book form and were read by people throughout America and much of Europe. A fury of protest erupted because nineteenth-century Christians did not accept the idea of perfectionism.

The evangelist, however, had come by his teaching honestly. He always searched for truth, and regarding his idea of perfectionism, he declared, "I say again that true Christian consistency implies progress in knowledge and holiness, and such changes in theory and in practice as are demanded by increasing light." Further, Charles could be tenacious in clinging to his beliefs: "If upon further discussion and investigation I see no cause to change, I hold them [new ideas] fast."

Certain conditions that Charles had witnessed led to a search for a higher Christian life. Initially, he realized after finishing a series of meetings, a number of believers would digress into a state of spiritual stagnation. Older church members seemed more inclined to stagnate than new converts. Also, Charles admitted concerning his own Christian life:

> *I was also led into a state of great dissatisfaction with my own want of stability in faith and love. To be candid, and tell the truth, I must say, to the praise of God's grace, He did not suffer me to backslide, to anything like the same extent, to which manifestly many Christians did backslide. But I often felt myself weak in the presence of temptation; and needed frequently to hold days of fasting and prayer, and to spend much time in overhauling my own religious life, in order to retain that communion with God, and that hold upon the divine strength, that would enable me efficiently to labor.*

Another area that concerned Charles was the quality of life in the church itself. Could there not be something better and more lasting than the majority of Christians knew about—even those whose Christian consecration and maturity seemed evident? Thus he asked the question: "Was there not means provided in the gospel, for the establishment of Christians in altogether a higher form of Christian life?"

Numerous individuals agreed with Charles's point of view expressed in the "Lectures to Professing Christians" and were greatly helped by his ideas. He told of his own experience of divine blessing:

> *The last winter that I spent in New York, the*
> *Lord was pleased to visit my soul with a great*
> *refreshing. After a season of great searching of*
> *heart, He brought me, as He has often done,*
> *into a large place, and gave me much of that*
> *divine sweetness in my soul, of which President*
> *[Jonathan] Edwards speaks as he has attained*
> *in his own experience. That winter I had a thor-*
> *ough breaking up: so much so that sometimes,*
> *for a considerable period, I could not refrain*
> *from loud weeping in view of my own sins, and*
> *of the love of God in Christ. Such seasons were*
> *frequent that winter, and resulted in the great*
> *renewal of my spiritual strength, and enlarge-*
> *ment of my views in regard to the privileges*
> *of Christians, and the abundance of the grace*
> *of God.*

Some of the hue and cry that came forth from more traditional Christians was that Charles's view bordered on
heresy; further, the view was considered antinomian. If
the evangelist's view was the right one, and a person was
perfect, he could live any way he wished.

After much opposition by various churches and leading ecclesiastical authorities, "Oberlin Perfectionism" was
called as an item to be discussed before a convention in
Cleveland. Lyman Beecher, the evangelist's main oppo-
nent in the "new measures" fracas, turned out to be the
chief adversary this time as well. Charles never refuted his
position, but neither did he criticize his opponents' stance.
He did experience much ostracism from certain quarters;

moreover, the Oberlin Institute published two periodicals reflecting Charles's (and Mahan's) views: the *Oberlin Evangelist*, and later, the *Oberlin Quarterly*. These publications reached many people with the evangelist's ideas and also preserved much of his writing.

Overall, Charles's years at Oberlin were fruitful ones—for himself and for his students. As a theology professor, he had to study long and hard to stay ahead of his students; but in the process of applying theological concepts to real life, he grew and matured in his faith along with the students. His practicality served him well, too, as he advised the students on many everyday matters. He told them, for example, "Beware how you write ladies; what is written is written." He cautioned future ministers not to blow their noses with their fingers, not to spit on the carpet, and not to use dirty handkerchiefs.

Other disgusting habits they should not practice were: not to put their feet and muddy boots on the sofa or on the door posts, nor to pull off their socks in front of families. He related two revolting stories to classes. The first concerned a young minister "who called on some ladies after walking some distance, took off his boots and hung his socks on the andirons the first thing."

Another minister, according to the theology professor, "Put his feet up in a window in a lady's parlor to enjoy the cool air." Some other habits Charles advocated for his students were to practice good grooming by keeping their nails and hair clean and being sure they had clean teeth and sweet breath. Most of these students had grown up on the frontier and needed to be taught about good hygiene.

The evangelist provided an excellent model for his students to emulate. They did so; whether Charles taught in the classroom, where they could see his earnestness and determination to live for Christ, or whether they observed him preaching with utmost conviction as pastor of the Oberlin Congregational Church. The Oberlin Institute, however, could not expect their famous professor-preacher to give them all his time. The world at large still needed him, too. So Charles set his sights once more toward his calling as a preacher of revivals.

fifteen

By the winter of 1842, Oberlin Institute enjoyed new peace and optimism. The furor over perfectionism had died down, but also the school's stance on abolition and even being a station in the underground railway for runaway slaves had become much more palatable to the surrounding areas, and especially to the State of Ohio itself. The anger of Northerners had exploded as they watched slave owners attempting to retrieve their slaves. Seeing the evils of slavery firsthand caused them to look on Oberlin with more favorable eyes.

Because of the stability at the institute, Charles was able to answer a new call to preach in Boston, where a special chapel had been prepared for him. A close friend, Willard Sears, had bought the Marlborough Hotel in Boston and renovated it into a large chapel where services could be held. Several religious crosscurrents, such as the Adventist Movement, had led to confusion among

Bostonians. As the evangelist preached, he noted that "the Spirit of the Lord was immediately poured out." Under conviction for sin, people continuously knocked on his door seeking peace, and many soon came to a personal knowledge of Christ.

From Boston, the evangelist was called to Providence, Rhode Island, by Josiah Chapin, a large contributor to Oberlin Institute. Charles was thrilled at the conversions of many prominent citizens. A judge of the Supreme Court, who was a well-known skeptic, began attending the services. The man paid close attention to the services even though he had not come to them before. One night as the evangelist closed his message, the old judge stood up asking if he might say something to the people. Charles told him he could, and choking with emotion, the judge said:

> *My friends and neighbors, you are probably surprised to see me attend these meetings. You have known my skeptical views, and that I have not been in the habit of attending religious meetings, for a long time. But hearing of the state of things in this congregation, I came in here; and I wish to have my friends and neighbors know that I believe that the preaching we are hearing, from night to night, is the gospel. I have altered my mind. I believe this is the truth, and the true way of salvation. I say this that you may understand my real motive for coming here; that it is not to criticize and find fault, but to attend to the great question of salvation, and to encourage others to attend to it.*

The feeling with which the judge spoke greatly affected the congregation, and many others came under conviction. Charles continued to hold nightly inquiry meetings in the large basement room below the church. Night after night, the room filled to overflowing. Again, the evangelist rejoiced in the pouring out of God's Spirit on Providence.

By spring, it was time for Charles to return to Oberlin. On his way, he rested for a day in Rochester, New York, with a friend. But when word got out that he was in their area, a leading judge in the state court of appeals urged him to stay and preach. Several others prevailed on him as well. The evangelist always found it difficult to say no, so he remained in Rochester.

Charles did most of his preaching in George S. Boardman's Bethel Church. As the meetings got under way, several attorneys asked him to preach a series of sermons to the city's lawyers. The evangelist rose to the occasion. Given his background as a lawyer, he relished the opportunity to persuade his peers about the truth of the gospel. He knew their skeptical bent, but he knew, too, their love of argumentation. In his first message to the attorneys, Charles asked, "Do we know anything?" He began to build his arguments on what is known. Of course, many of those who were not lawyers failed to appreciate some of these messages, yet the church was filled to capacity every night.

For two months, Charles preached in Rochester. The meetings increased in fervency and impact. The whole city was soon moved by his meetings. Each denomination in the city profited from the revival. More than one thousand conversions took place throughout the city. Many of this number were attorneys—and some of them chose to enter the Christian ministry later. A number of physicians found Christ, too.

Charles believed that lawyers proved easier to reach than physicians because of the latter group's skeptical turn of mind. Of lawyers, he said: "I have always found, wherever I have labored, that when the gospel was properly presented, they were the most accessible class of men; and I believe it is true that, in proportion to their relative number, in any community, more have been converted, than of any other class." As for physicians, he did concede, "They are intelligent; if the gospel is thoroughly set before them, they are easily convinced."

Following the Rochester revival, Charles traveled back to Oberlin for the summer session. Then, in the fall of 1843, he returned to Boston and Marlborough Chapel. His earlier ministry of the year before had not really settled the prevailing religious controversies. Charles remarked: "Their system is one of denials. Their theology is negative. They deny almost everything, and affirm almost nothing." The evangelist believed the Unitarians were largely to blame for the situation since they caused the orthodox to question every doctrine of the Christian faith.

As Charles struggled with the religious turmoil and faced small attendance and few visible results, he also faced a personal crisis. He struggled over his own dedication and holiness. Moreover, the lethargy and lack of spirituality of many church members troubled him. He turned to prayer. When the evening services were finished, he would retire at once so he could arise at four in the morning to pray. Then he would be so caught up in intercession that he would still be praying on his knees when called for breakfast at eight o'clock. After breakfast, he would return to his room and spend the rest of the day reading the Scriptures. He read nothing but the Bible during that time and with wonder exclaimed, "The whole Scripture seemed to me all ablaze with light."

He continued in these pursuits for weeks and months. He made a surrender and commitment to God that was more complete than any other he had known. His understanding of complete consecration went beyond what he had thought possible. Now, God allowed him to be tested, and the test involved his beloved wife, Lydia.

Though Charles had often surrendered his family to the perfect will of God, this time it was different. Lydia lay very ill back in Ohio and had only a short time to live. Charles struggled over giving her up. He revealed his anguish with these words:

I wrote to my wife, telling her what a struggle I had had, and the concern that I had felt at not being willing to commit her, without reserve to the perfect will of God. But I was able, after struggling for a few moments with this discouragement and bitterness, which I have since attributed to a fiery dart of Satan, to fall back, in a deeper sense than I had ever done before upon the infinitely blessed and perfect will of God. I then told the Lord that I had such

> *confidence in Him, that I felt perfectly willing to*
> *give myself, my wife and my family, all to be*
> *disposed of according to His own wisdom.*

Following this experience, the evangelist experienced a wonderful victory. He had given his beloved wife up to the perfect will of God and now experienced an abiding peace. He had a new "holy boldness," and said that his "mind settled into a perfect stillness." A great joy pervaded his soul along with an intense desire for God's will to be done on earth as it is in heaven.

God had prepared Charles for Lydia's death in December of 1847. Although it was difficult initially for him, Charles again surrendered himself to God's perfect will. Almost a year later, in November of 1848, Charles married a widow, Mrs. Elizabeth Ford Atkinson of Rochester, New York. One chapter had closed in his life; a new one was about to begin.

sixteen

After receiving numerous invitations to visit England, Charles and his new wife left for Southampton in early November 1849, almost a year after their marriage. The evangelist was glad to leave the turmoil of pre–Civil War problems behind and travel to a place of relative calm. He knew that his *Lectures on Revival of Religion* had preceded him and been warmly received and that many revivals had occurred as a result. He anticipated an enthusiastic welcome.

The Finneys were to be guests of Potto Brown, a Quaker and a wealthy layman in Houghton, a small town in the south midlands. Mr. Brown's partner had died a year earlier and left six children. Brown had taken the children into his home, but not one of the children had been converted to Christ. During the time that Charles ministered in Houghton, however, the Brown home became a center for inquirers and friends of the Finneys.

Large numbers of people came and enjoyed fellowship and meals with the Finneys.

Before long each of Brown's adopted children had come to Christ. Of course, many of the inquirers also came to a knowledge of Christ, and joy began to spread throughout the community. The *Oberlin Evangelist*, in Ohio, reported the wonderful success of Charles's work in England: "We learn that Professor Finney's first labors in England have been chiefly in Houghton for a period of about three weeks, and signally successful. People have come in from a distance of forty miles to attend the meetings, and many are turned to the Lord. The state of things there is said to be very much as it was in this country twenty years ago." In addition, the publication wrote that "Mrs. Finney is with her husband, abundant in labors, and jointly with him requests the prayers of Christian friends."

After a three-week stay in Houghton, the Finneys moved on to Birmingham, where Charles preached in Carr's Lane Church, pastored by the Reverend John Angell James. James had written the introduction for Finney's British edition of *Lectures on Revivals of Religion*.

In Birmingham, the evangelist learned of several critical letters complaining of theological errors. As usual, Charles met the criticism head on by inviting a number of ministers for breakfast and an open discussion on the questionable points. He also gave James a copy of his *Lectures on Systematic Theology* so he would know where the evangelist stood on different issues.

Charles also gave a copy of his book to Dr. George Redford, a well-respected British theologian. After reviewing the book, neither of these men had any serious objections. Dr. Redford concluded, "I see no reason for regarding Mr. Finney, in any respect, as unsound. He has his own way of stating theological propositions; but I cannot see that he differs on any essential point, from us."

With the way cleared of any possible theological differences, the evangelist was ready to move ahead. The methods he used in Britain were, as he noted, "The same that I had done in [America]. Preaching, prayer, conversation and meetings of inquiry." Numerous people again called on the Finneys to inquire about the salvation of their souls and to fellowship. The Spirit of God again sent revival.

The people in Oberlin had hope that Charles would be able to visit what Americans considered the queen of cities, London. In answer to prayer, Dr. John Campbell, editor of the *British Banner* and a successor to George Whitefield in the London Tabernacle, wrote Charles: "You are aware that it pleased God, now a century ago, through the instrumentality of an Englishman to bless America; and who can but tell it may please Him, by means of an American to bless England?" Campbell referred, of course, to George Whitefield, who had had a huge ministry in what were then the British colonies. In response to his invitation, the Finneys set off for London in May 1850.

Charles preached in the London Tabernacle for several weeks. Inquiry meetings became regular events during the London revival, and the evangelist would call for people to stand to receive Christ. There was not room for them to come forward. Sometimes as many as two thousand people rose in response to the invitation. People came from every part of the city and from miles around. The crowd would sit spellbound as Charles preached for one and a half hours. The *British Banner* stated that the people would gladly have heard Charles speak throughout the night.

Mrs. Finney took part in the women's movement during the revival meetings. Such meetings were a brand new thing for the people of London. At first, she did not assume a large leadership role, but Dr. Campbell asked her to help one day in what the Londoners called "tea meetings" for poor, uneducated women. She was expected to lead the service, and she assumed the men who were present would leave when the meeting began. At that time, women did not speak to groups that included adult men. However, the men stayed, and Mrs. Finney, characteristically like her husband, rose to the occasion and spoke to the group for forty-five minutes. Following this breakthrough, Mrs. Finney continued to take a more prominent part in the meetings.

After preaching for several months in England, Charles was summoned back to Oberlin. He sensed that he should stay in England because of widespread revival, but discontent was increasing in Ohio due to his absence and problems that were developing with the Oberlin presidency. Reluctantly, Charles agreed to return, but he promised the English he would come back, which he did in December 1858. The second time the evangelist preached, he was as warmly received as the first time.

On his second trip to England, Charles ministered in

some new places such as Scotland, Manchester, and Lancashire. By Christmas 1859, the Finneys were ministering in Bolton, a town of thirty thousand located several miles from Manchester. While in Bolton, Charles encouraged those attending the meetings to go out two by two and canvas each home in the town with the gospel message. This was his latest new measure. As the Finneys prepared to leave Bolton, the citizens presented them with a lovely paper which stated:

Rev. and Dear Sir; It is with deep regret, but also with cordial feeling and devout gratitude to the Father of mercies and God of all grace, that we assemble and bid you "Farewell" at the close of your arduous labors in our midst. We own the Providence which directed your steps to our town, and we feel that we can never cease to be your debtors for the earnest and self-sacrificing efforts which you have made, while with us, to deepen the spiritual life in our own hearts, to increase our devotion and enjoyment of the gospel, to secure the salvation of our friends, and to extend the Redeemer's kingdom in this important and densely populated district. Wherever you go, we will follow you with our earnest prayers and deepest sympathies. May you be long spared to labor, and after you have finished your course with joy, may you receive the crown of life that fadeth not away, and shines as the brightness of the firmament in the kingdom of our Father forever and ever.

As the Finneys left England on August 2, 1860, they were tired. They had worked long and hard throughout the nation and needed to return to Oberlin for some much-deserved rest.

seventeen

No longer an insignificant wilderness college, Oberlin Institute had grown considerably by the 1850s. The student body alone had increased from 101 students in 1835 to 484 in 1840.

The Oberlin trustees had asked Charles to assume the presidency of the college after the resignation of Asa Mahan. He accepted with some reluctance, but he realized, as the trustees assured him, that Oberlin needed his energy in its highest office. He would be able to continue pastoring the Congregational church in Oberlin and maintain his professorship as well.

When Charles became president in 1851, the college had grown to 1,020 students. The evangelist's rapport with the students proved to be warm and friendly, and his sense of humor greatly appealed to young people. One evening after Charles had invited his class to his home for a lecture, a student fell asleep in a comfortable chair. As the professor finished lecturing his class, he prayed, asking God to keep the class interested enough so that they would be able to stay awake.

When the group returned for another lecture the following day, however, they discovered the room had been filled with wooden, straight-backed chairs from the kitchen. With a twinkle in his eye, Charles told them, "You see, young gentlemen, I have found a way to answer my own prayer."

Not only did Charles have the love and respect of his students, but the townspeople admired him, too. He, in turn, expressed interest in their concerns. In the summer of 1853 when the northern Ohio farmers were experiencing a terrible drought, Charles offered a prayer in church for the situation:

Lord, we want rain. We do not presume to dictate unto Thee, but our pastures are dry, and the earth is gaping open for rain. The cattle are wandering about and lowing in search of water. Even the little squirrels in the woods are suffering from thirst. Unless Thou givest us rain, our cattle will die and our harvests will come to naught. O Lord, send us rain, and send it now! Although to us there is no sign of it, it is an easy thing for Thee to do. Send it now, for Christ's sake. Amen.

Before the service ended, the rain began to fall in such torrents that the preacher could scarcely be heard. Charles paused, and urged, "Let us praise God for this rain." He also suggested they sing a hymn:

When all thy mercies, O my God,
  My rising soul surveys,
Transported with the view, I'm lost
  In wonder, love and praise.

Many in the congregation were unable to sing because of their tears. God was still at work on the Oberlin campus.

Charles endured various trials during the 1860s and 1870s. The first one was the death of his second wife on November 27, 1863. Elizabeth Finney had been a great contributor to the evangelist's ministry as she led women's prayer meetings and other meetings. Charles was filled with profound loss at her death. The Lord had taught him, however, to face sorrow.

The second happened when, at age seventy-five, his health broke down. This event forced the evangelist to rest completely for some time. Others had to carry on the revival work he had started on the Oberlin campus.

In 1864, the Lord brought Charles another wife, Miss Rebecca A. Rayl. She had been the assistant principal of the ladies' department at Oberlin. Rebecca Finney died in Kentland, Indiana, on September 12, 1907. She survived her husband by thirty-two years.

Although invitations to hold meetings continued to come to him, Charles decided that his health was not good enough to sustain the work involved in such meetings. Even the work of the college presidency was becoming more than he could handle. So in August 1865, Charles resigned the presidency. He continued to pastor the church, but in 1872, when he was almost eighty, he resigned from the pastorate as well.

His time on earth was drawing to a close. Charles had served his Lord faithfully for several decades and been instrumental in countless revivals and souls coming to Christ. His preaching, with its many innovations, provided an entirely new pattern for evangelism. His call for immediate repentance was revolutionary. One contemporary said of him:

> *Mr. Finney is one of the most remarkable*
> *preachers in America. His strong logical powers,*
> *and educated as a lawyer, he deals much in con-*
> *vincing argument. He preaches more the love of*
> *God, and wins as well as alarms to repentance.*
> *His strength of mind is equalled by that of*
> *few; for a certain scope of preaching he is*
> *unequalled—that of impressive argument, and*
> *such presenting of the relations of religious*
> *truth as in its completeness and clearness works*
> *irresistible conviction, and brings skeptic,*
> *infidel, and atheist alike into broken hearted*
> *submission to the power of God.*

Further, Charles proved to be a talented and effective reformer. His view of the gospel compelled him to speak out on many of the social issues of his day; abolition, women's rights, racism, and temperance were all touched on by his ministry as he sought to deal with people fairly, according to God's Word.

His writings, in particular, spread his ideas worldwide.

His *Lectures on Revivals of Religion* was instrumental in bringing revivals to many parts of the world. Also, his *Memoirs, Systematic Theology,* and *Lectures to Professing Christians* reveal his deep thinking on religious subjects. The work Charles did with the Oberlin students had a long-lasting effect on their lives and ministries as they sought to emulate him.

Undoubtedly, Charles's greatest contribution was that of a revival evangelist. The new measures he used to promote the cause of Christ have stood the test of time. The use of prayer meetings for revivals; the call for a public response to receive Christ; the personalizing of the salvation message; the counseling of inquirers; the protracted, structured, and organized meeting; and the use of any suitable building to preach the gospel are among his greatest achievements.

Charles Finney's evangelistic ministry provides a pivotal link between Jonathan Edwards of the First Great Awakening and Dwight L. Moody, who preached worldwide revivals in the mid- to late-1800s. One of Charles's critics, B. B. Warfield of Princeton, even conceded that Charles "conducted the most spectacular evangelism activities the country has ever witnessed."

Scotland's David Livingstone was one of the international Christian leaders who benefitted from the evangelist's ministry. In 1839, while preparing to go to Africa, he sent the first pay he received to his younger brother, urging him to study under Finney at Oberlin. Livingstone's brother heeded the advice and graduated from Oberlin in 1845.

Charles Finney gave his last series of lectures to

Oberlin in July 1875, when he was eighty-two years old. His erect posture, demeanor, and bearing seemed that of a younger man. Then in August of that year, he preached once more at his beloved First Congregational Church of Oberlin. His piercing eyes penetrated wherever they glanced. The congregation sat in quiet awe of his spiritual power and keen insight into the Christian life.

On Sunday, August 15, 1875, Charles spent a quiet day with his wife. They thought of God's goodness and faithfulness. At sunset they strolled over to linger near the old church and listen to the singing. They joined in as the congregation sang, "Jesus, Lover of My Soul." The words went straight to Charles's heart as he remembered the long-ago day of October 10, 1821, when salvation's truth had first pierced his soul. When the hymn faded away, the Finneys walked back home and retired for the evening.

About two o'clock in the morning, the evangelist experienced severe chest pains. His wife got up, and shortly, some friends gathered. Charles asked for water, but his thirst could not be satisfied. In his pain, as he looked at the anxious eyes around the bed, he said softly, "Perhaps this is the thirst of death."

A moment or two later, he added, "I am dying." He closed his eyes. Although he lingered a few more hours, those were his last words. As the dawn began to break forth that August morning, Charles breathed his last breath and passed on to his heavenly reward. At last he was home and joined the multitudes of others he had brought to Christ.

His son, Frederick Norton Finney, had inscribed in

the vestibule of the Oberlin College Chapel these words
as a tribute to his father:

THAT THE YOUTH
OF THIS FOUNDATION OF LEARNING
MAY DAILY MEET TO WORSHIP GOD
AND THAT A SON MAY HONOUR
THE MEMORY OF HIS FATHER
THIS CHAPEL IS BUILT
TO
CHARLES GRANDISON FINNEY
BY
HIS YOUNGEST SON
FREDERICK NORTON FINNEY
In the Year of Our Lord
1908

Bibliography

Drummond, Lewis A. *The Life and Ministry of Charles G. Finney*. Minneapolis, MN: Bethany House Publishers, 1983.

Edman, V. Raymond. *Finney Lives On*. New York: Fleming H. Revell Co., 1951.

Finney, Charles G. *Lectures on Revival*. Minneapolis, MN: Bethany House Publishers, 1988.

Finney, Charles G. *Memoirs*. New York: Fleming H. Revell Co., 1908.

Hardesty, Nancy A. *Your Daughters Shall Prophesy*. Brooklyn, NY: Carlson Publishing, Inc., 1991.

Harding, William Henry. *Finney's Life and Lectures*. Grand Rapids, MI: Zondervan Publishing House, 1956.

Weddle, David L. *The Law as Gospel*. Metuchen, NJ: The Scarecrow Press, Inc., 1985.

HEROES OF THE FAITH